STUDIES IN FORMAL HISTORICAL LINGUISTICS

FORMAL LINGUISTICS SERIES

Editor:

H. HIŻ, *University of Pennsylvania*

Consulting Editors:

ZELLIG S. HARRIS, *University of Pennsylvania*

HENRY M. HOENIGSWALD, *University of Pennsylvania*

VOLUME 3

HENRY M. HOENIGSWALD

STUDIES IN FORMAL
HISTORICAL LINGUISTICS

D. REIDEL PUBLISHING COMPANY

DORDRECHT-HOLLAND / BOSTON-U.S.A.

Library of Congress Catalog Card Number 72–95891

ISBN 90 277 0270 5

Published by D. Reidel Publishing Company,
P.O. Box 17, Dordrecht, Holland

Sold and distributed in the U.S.A., Canada, and Mexico
by D. Reidel Publishing Company, Inc.
306 Dartmouth Street, Boston,
Mass. 02116, U.S.A.

Printed in The Netherlands by D. Reidel, Dordrecht

For GSH

PREFACE

These separate but related essays owe their existence to a combined concern for the workings of text criticism and historical linguistics and for the history of scholarship in these fields. On earlier occasions I have suggested certain views on the development of the so-called comparative method. Few things are more rewarding than to bring implicit preconceptions of the past and present out into the open, as I aimed to do then and as I aim to do now. This time existing tradition is treated as a body – without, I hope, being seriously distorting – and one small portion of its working assumptions is examined.

My thanks go to the colleagues and students with whom I have had fruitful discussion, but especially to Zellig S. Harris, and to Henry Hiż who expended much more than just his excellent editorial care on these efforts. I only hope that I have learned as much from him as he has patiently tried to teach me.

Lloyd W. Daly has kindly read parts of an earlier version and has contributed valuable suggestions.

H.M.H.

PRELIMINARY NOTE

The relationship between historical linguistics and its humanistic sisters has been complex and subtle. What set historical linguistics apart almost from its modern beginnings was a formalistic bent which was by no means always gladly professed but which in fact became more and more pronounced as time went on. At least since Schleicher, primary work along historical and 'comparative' lines (primary as distinct from the more derivative efforts to codify it and to define its standing with regard to other disciplines) has been concentrated in areas that are particularly amenable to formal procedures. There were rewards: in the event, methodological clarity and consistency was seen to pay off in the form of coherent and sometimes testable results. There are other humanistic fields, to be sure, to which considerations of this sort are not entirely alien. Notably this is true of textual criticism, and it is interesting that the historian of philology and linguistics can detect some of the academic and biographical ties that went back and forth among the practitioners of those parallel disciplines. There are procedural analogies between the approach which made Karl Lachmann's name famous, on the one hand, and the later development of linguistic reconstruction, on the other. There are indications now that these analogies may go a good deal beyond the world of languages and manuscripts and may embrace other processes which occur in prehistoric, even geological and cosmic, time.

If the scholarly record contains those formal linguistic factors in some indirect fashion only, this is a challenge to make them explicit. Sometimes indirect mention consists in an impatient and disdainful hint that such and such an interpretation or inference is obvious and inescapable, not on some factual grounds, but on grounds of logic. It is implied that other choices would lead to internal contradiction, or be meaningless. Sometimes the hint is well-founded, especially when it is given in a concrete context in which the investigator has explicitly or intuitively tested the alternatives. Whether or not this is sufficient is a matter of preference or, perhaps, strategy. Procedures and principles in linguistics are best developed in close touch with nature. Some of the greatest linguists have, in fact, thought it more important to develop than to formulate them, and many great linguists have had better success developing than formulating. Yet, there are situations in dealing with natural data – polemical situations, in particular – in which a statement of principles saves waste and leads to the realization that certain factual problems were ill-formulated; or that some factual problems are related to other factual problems as special, or as more general, cases. If formalization needs a defense, this would be part of it.

Much of the uncertainty in historical linguistics centers on the concept of the change event. It is easier to understand the relation between whole linguistic systems – successive stages; related languages – than to isolate particular historical events the sum total of which produces the systemic difference. (It will be suggested in the following pages that this parallels a familiar difficulty in synchronic work: the segmentation of the flow of speech is still a major theoretical problem.) It might be best if the notion of 'one change event' could somehow be abandoned. But it so happens that formal statements, or rather hints at an existing formal necessity of a sort that would be decisive in favor of one over another interpretation of language history, are most often made about such allegedly discrete events and their relative position in time. The student of past forms of language frequently meets this problem in a special way. He sees two languages, decides that they may be stages of 'one' language, and begins to try to bring order into the differences between them. What gives him the right to isolate events and order them? One thing is certain: the identification of the several steps and their ordering are not independent of each other.

In particular, it would be important to understand by what reasoning scholars will reconstruct 'intermediate' stages when such stages are not given. Some of this is here attempted. It is done in a spirit of recognizing preconceptions and, perhaps, prejudices, and not of devising some sure road to historical truth. One soon learns that certain formal principles, appealed to indirectly perhaps, but with an implication of evident validity, are less cogent than they are claimed to be. And yet the practices and concrete interpretations which they are designed to buttress do stand up as reasonable and, on occasion, as verifiable. The first essay is devoted to this discussion.

The scope of the second and third essay is narrower. In both the subject matter is trees of descent; but a number of much-labored problems pertaining to such trees are not touched. One is the appropriateness of the very tree model to language history. It is well known that this appropriateness is limited and that there may not be any situations in history where 'clear cleavage' of the kind which makes the tree an adequate representation of what happened occurred in all purity. Then the question is only whether the model is still useful in those situations in which clear cleavage is approximated; pragmatic tests of this are rather encouraging. The other problem is that of evidence in glottochronology. The statistical standing of the glottochronological, and in particular lexicostatistical, parameters has recently been scrutinized again by Sankoff (1973). But on a less technical level there is, after all, the not unreasonable belief in the existence of some factor (amenable to quantification) which is correlated to the remoteness, either by ancestry and descent or collaterally, among related languages. On these hypothetical but not exactly irrational grounds we ask, in the third essay, certain questions about the glottochronological properties to be expected in languages which form given trees of descent of the more familiar, classical type. Some important points of this type are, of course, treated in the work of Dyen *et al.* (e.g., 1967). In any event, the term 'glottochronology' is here used in a wide sense; it is not meant to cover the specific efforts that have been made to find a reliable parameter, such as basic vocabulary loss, to measure time depths.

To return briefly to the subject of the second essay: the comparison between linguistic and textual stemmata is a special challenge, since there are in existence excellent formalizations, as well as excellent discursive statements, of textual reconstruction. Particular tribute must be paid to the works, referred to below, by Greg (1927) and Maas (1960) – each reflecting in a most interesting way the different traditions of the two fields of scholarship in which those two men moved, English studies and the Greek and Latin classics, respectively. One mentions their names with trepidation, both because of their general stature and for one special reason. Both Greg and Maas, but Greg in particular, were outspoken on the formally degenerate nature of the very object to which we address ourselves here: the three-witness tree. They were right: three manuscripts, or three related languages, are not sufficient to allow a good many of the more important generalizations. For this reason as for others, the scope of the second chapter, like that of the third, remains limited.

TABLE OF CONTENTS

CHAPTER I

ON THE NOTION OF AN INTERMEDIATE STAGE
IN TRADITIONAL HISTORICAL LINGUISTICS

1. Sound change, as classically thought of, is stated in a characteristic form, namely in terms of replacement, for instance:[1] IE $d >$ E t; IE $r >$ E r; IE $st >$ E st, or alternatively, IE $s > s/-t$; IE $t > t/s-$ (read: IE s before t, yields or remains s; IE t after s, yields or remains t); OE $\#kn >$ NE $\#n$, or, alternatively, OE $_\#k_n >$ NE $_\# \oslash_n$, OE$k > \oslash / \# -n$ (read: yields zero, is dropped, becomes silent), OE $n >$ NE n. More generally, I $a/1 >$ II $m/101$, where I = older stage, II = later stage; a = an element of the older stage, m = an element of the later stage; 1, 2 = environments stated in terms of elements of the older stage (a, b, c,...); 101, 102 = environments stated in terms of elements of the later stage (m, n, o, ...) in a certain order; in addition to the position '$-$' with regard to which the environment occurs.[2] Some of the factors named need further discussion.

2. Stage I and II each are collections of discourses, possibly datable, recorded in a phonological alphabet (for I: a, b, c,...; for II: m, n, o,...).[3] Traditionally, such an alphabet is often, or is often close to, a so-called autonomous phonemic notation of a kind which records homonymies (e.g. Mod. German *búnt* both for '*Bund*' and '*bunt*') and makes more or less arbitrary choices in situations of redundancy or neutralization (*búnt*, not *búnd*, even though *t* does not 'contrast' with *d* before $\#$).[4] The choices are sometimes said to be made on the basis of 'phonetic similarity' whenever they can be so made: the *t* of *búnt* is more similar, perhaps in the sense that it shares more features with the *t* of *búnte* '*bunte*' than with the *d* of *búnde* '*Bunde*'. In this case the property of markedness might be attributed to the recessive partner, *d*.[5]

3. There is, however, no reason why other types of notation could not also be employed. The merits of other choices will, in fact, appear later (Sections 14–5). In the interest of maintaining continuity with the work of the past which it is our aim to comment upon it will be well to adhere to two requirements: a weaker one, that discourses judged by speakers as different not be represented as being alike; and a stronger, homonymy-serving one, that discourses judged identical be represented in one and the same way.[6] This leaves room for a variety of mutually convertible styles. Consider that there are probably consistently observed physical differences at any point ('seg-

ment') in time between utterances of *hens* on the one hand, and *hence* on the other:[7] differences in duration, relative voicing of both 'the *n*' and 'the *s/c*'. It is not necessary here to justify the custom of considering the distinctive difference between the two as lodged in the end portions of the utterances, with the other differences determined by it. Much discussion of phonemics has turned around arguments for preferring one segmentation (and one corresponding use of an alphabet) to another.

4.   It is a consequence of the homonym-preserving principle embodied in biunique, autonomous notation that morpheme boundaries are not expressed in it, although 'junctures', that is alleged features of onset, release, syllabication, etc., for the proper recording of which a pseudo-segment is constructed, may be so expressed. On the other hand, the incidence of morpheme boundaries is of importance for the understanding of sound change. Texts may therefore be envisaged as being recorded in some biunique phonemic alphabet, with added information on their morphological segmentation.

5.   Each alphabetical symbol, or each 'phoneme' for which it stands, has its distributional range, that is, the collection of all the discourse-long environments in which it occurs. This notion may be open to criticism more severe than the mere unfeasibility of recording 'all' ranges justifies. But with some limitation (governed, no doubt, by considerations of phonetic naturalness or of phonetic universals) to short-range context – say, of syllable length – the determination of environmental range is possible, and is needed for a relevant description. Since it is true that no two phonemic entities should normally have identical ranges, inasmuch as they would then be totally interchangeable and hence reduced to 'free variants', (any more than two entities can have mutually exclusive ranges and not be potential positional variants), a given phonemic entity may be regarded as characterized by the range of its environments. In English, *t* is that phoneme the frames for which include $\#s-$Vowel and $\#s-r$, but not $\#s-l$.

6.   Any alphabet must also be thought of as comprising the element ⌀, signifying 'nothing' or 'contact'. Thus, instead of *ab* we may wish to write *a*⌀*b*, and indeed *a*⌀⌀*b*, *a*⌀⌀⌀*b*, *a*⌀⌀⌀... *b*. Note that ⌀ ('nothing') has a statable range: if the sequence *ab* occurs, i.e. if the range of *a* includes $-b$, and that of *b* includes $a-$, then ⌀ may be said to occur in the environment $a-b$. If *cd* fails to occur, ⌀ may be said not to occur in the environment $c-d$.[8] In this sense ⌀ may be said to contrast with a 'real' entity

e if both *aeb* and *ab*, i.e. *a*⊘*b*, occur in what are, in turn, their characteristic environment ranges.[9]

7.   All entities written by symbols, including ⊘, may thus be seen as characterized by their mutual cooccurrence in discourses.[10] This is true for each stage, I and II, separately. Our use of separate sets of letters for each (*a* to *l* for I; *m* to *w* for II) is an expression of this. Necessary, or at least natural and perhaps desirable, compromising with the writing historically used in extant texts (for instance, the Roman alphabet for OE and NE) often leads to partial use of the same symbols for both stages. Typically, two kinds of reality are behind this practice: (1) identity of distinctive-feature properties under some universal inventory of such features (e.g., OE *k* and NE *k* are probably, in that sense, identical); and (2) homology in a distributional sense (e.g., OE *k*, like NE *k*, contrasts with dentals, palatals, labials; but note also that among voiceless obstruents OE *k* may be defined as the one which occurs in # − *n*, which is not true of NE *k* with regard to NE # − *n*, and that by the same token such identity cannot even be attributed to the two ⊘s of I and II respectively, since the replacement OE # ⊘*k*⊘*n*> > NE# ⊘*n* imparts a new (and smaller) range not only to *k* and to *n* but to ⊘ as well). In any event the replacement relation between *a* and *m* is independent of the other relations just discussed, though all may be considered in combination. Thus if *m* both shares its distinctive feature properties with *a* and replaces *a*, it is traditional to say (with use of the same alphabet for both stages) that *a* 'remains' *a*.

8.   It is generally held that any two languages are translatable into each other. Presumably there exists a theory of translation. Such a theory may be expected to have something to say about formal relationships between discourses (and their constituents) and their translations in the other language. We can here only operate with the notion that for any meaningful string in one language there are acceptable translations, in the form of meaningful strings, in the other.

9.   In addition to their defining relationship, texts and their translations may exhibit certain regularities. Some of these interest the typologist and the student of potential language universals. Examples are: one-to-one translatability of morphemes that are semantically simple; one-to-one translatability of morphemes that are semantically complex, as when a pair of words forms a mutual translation both in a straight and in a metaphorical meaning; a sharing of grammatical categories, etc. But then, another variety of regularity stands out: the recurrence of phonological correspondences

among morphs that are translations of each other. In those extensive sectors of language where the arbitrariness of the linguistic sign is unimpaired – that is, outside, say, of onomatopoea and of parts of sentence intonation – such regularities are to be understood as products of specific history. Thus, if one language 'borrows' morphs from another under reasonably uniform conditions, chronologically and otherwise, there will be a non-random phonological pairing between the translations. Both h and $ḥ$ of Arabic words appear as h in Persian (in certain environments); both ' and ' (in certain environments) as ⵛ. The voiced hushing affricate of older French is reproduced by what is now E j in *judge*; when lexical items are borrowed from a later stage of French (into a later stage of English) the rendering is $ž$, as in *rouge*. These regularities obtain between the source language and the borrowing language, each reflecting a chronologically more or less well defined contact situation. Such regularities are compounded when two languages, having borrowed from a third, exhibit them.

10.   Both factual observation and prediction of a more speculative kind provide an explanation of this phenomenon as the result of 'sound substitution'. Usually acts of borrowing are considered secondary events, occurring against a background of primary internal sound change. Yet, the circumstance that such internal sound change is even better known to result in the same sort of phonological correspondence, between the older state I and the changed state II of the 'same' language, indicates a deeper connection between borrowing and sound change and suggests a factor in the causation of sound change.[11] There are certainly situations in which the distinction between a source of borrowing and an antecedent in sound change is difficult, and where it is better to speak simply of several channels of transmission, each one characterized by its own correspondences.

11.   It is, however, possible to distinguish between the following two kinds of relationship: one, in which one language is either a source of borrowing on the part of the other or an older stage of the other; and a second kind, in which the two languages are borrowers from, or descendants of, a third language. It is the 'comparative' method, applied to correspondences, which decides this.[12] If 'comparative' reconstruction from the two, or from particular correspondences within the two, yields a source identical with either, then the language with which the reconstruction is identical[13] is the source – that is, either the ancestor, or the model of the borrowing, as the case may be. If, on the other hand, the reconstruction differs from both languages, each proceeds separately from the reconstructed language.

12. It is usually assumed that there are typical and important differences between a principal channel of transmission and all other channels; in other words, that indigenous sound change can be told from borrowing, including 'dialect' borrowing, and that borrowing can be disregarded when sound change proper is discussed.[14] It is worth noting that descent (of a later stage or language from an older, under change), paradoxically, is a less primitive notion than is relationship, of which both collateral relationship and descent are special cases (Chapter 2, Section 5). The widespread impression to the contrary ('it is known that all language changes') is connected with the idea that a line of descent may be identified by inspection. But the identity of 'a' language through time is a problem, not a datum, whatever the customary labeling may seem to suggest. Scholars know that statements of the type: 'Modern English is the same language as Old English, except that it underwent change', or 'Italian is Latin as now spoken in Italy' are fraught with difficulties and that these difficulties can only be settled by recourse to the comparative method.[15]

13. Let us for a moment turn to the subject of distinctive features. This concept, while not openly developed in classical neogrammarian practice, was certainly implicit in the grid arrangements which neogrammarians were fond of using when describing sound systems synchronically, as well as in the terms for subsets of alphabetic elements that were used in the formulation of sound laws. Clearly, one part of Grimm's law is a statement about such things as 'voiced stops'; Latin vowel weakening affects a set of 'short vowels'; and so on.

14. Sometimes the claim is made that a true, natural distinctive feature notation constitutes the true, natural base for historical analysis and is thus preferable to the more usual near-segmental alphabets or tradition. It is not so certain, however, that the proper formulation of sound changes always calls for the same distinctive features to be isolated in the same manner. Take the Grimm-Verner complex. Among the entities affected, under the familiar formulation, are $p\ t\ k'\ k^w\ b\ d\ g'\ g^w$. Implicit in the equally familiar labeling of these older stage (reconstructed Indo-European) items as labials, dentals, palatals, labiovelars, voiceless and voiced stops is a distinctive feature division of sorts into four places and two manners of articulation,

	L	D	P	LV
vl	p	t	k'	k^w
vd	b	d	g'	g^w

Fig. 1.

or, if one prefers,[16]

	p	t	k'	k^w	b	d	g'	g^w
anterior	+	+	−	−	+	+	−	−
coronal	−	+	−	−	−	+	−	−
rounded	−	−	−	+	−	−	−	+
voiced	−	−	−	−	+	+	+	+

Fig. 2.

not to mention other possibilities.

Suppose that in some descendant a sound law converts k^w into p (we are using identical alphabets from stage to stage, employing the shortcut of Section 7), as well as g^w into b. Such pairs, or sets, of changes abound, and it may be said that the expression LV > L (in all environments, that is, not only before and after all segments but also in simultaneity with both vl and vd) is superior because it is 'simpler'. Or suppose that all $p>b$, all $t>d$, all $k'>g'$, and all $k^w>g^w$: the shorter statement would be vl > vd. Surely it does not matter how the relationship between phonetic basis and history is seen; whether we believe that history frequently operates in simple ways, or whether we have developed a hierarchy of ostensibly physical terms because they are in fact the appropriate ones for the purpose of formulating processes, both historical and synchronic.

15.   Now suppose, however, that $p>b$, $k'>g'$, $k^w>g^w$, while t 'remains' t – in other words, vl > vd in the 'environment' L, P, LV only. This might legitimately serve as an argument to order the four place-of-articulation properties into this three-step classification:

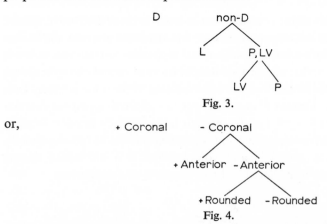

Fig. 3.

Fig. 4.

16.   Writing in historical linguistics abounds with statements to the effect that of two change events, usually phonological in nature, one must have

preceded the other. There is often a hint that such relative chronologies are founded on certain self-evident formal criteria and that any attempt at alternative orderings is bound to fail because of inherent contradictions. Indeed, those considerations are entirely internal; except that the results may (and should) converge, they have nothing to do with the relative chronologies obtained from the comparative method in cases where this method enables us to construct immediate, intermediate, and remote ancestors. The order in which the 'first' and the 'second' (or High German) consonant shift occurred in time follows from the fact that the stage ('West Germanic') antecedent to the 'second' shift is reconstructed from a subset of the languages which serve to reconstruct the stage ('Indo-European') antecedent to the 'first'. Such stages may be considered as 'known' history for purposes of analyzing internal reasoning. In fact, the study of internal relative chronology occupies a middle position between internal reconstruction in the accepted sense[17] and the more elementary task of following a line of descent which is directly accessible. In a typical problem, however, what is given are not two (or more) change events for which the true chronological succession is to be discovered; for the events in their discreteness are themselves chronological artifacts. Given are rather two outside stages, one initial and one final, with replacement relations such as, presumably, to call for the construction of an intermediate stage or intermediate stages. The challenge is to formulate both the stages AND their relative chronology.[18]

17. We formulate a simple model, of a type that will allow us to discuss some of the usual classical practices in intermediate-stage construction. Let there be an initial stage I which includes among its phonemes *s z r*; and let us think of these as contrasting rather fully (say, initially before vowels; between vowels; etc.), and also as sharing some distinctive features with one another. If, in fact, we visualize the three as (typologically, universally?) 'ordinary' *s*'s, *z*'s, and *r*'s, they might in some grid-like distinctive feature view be arrayed as follows:

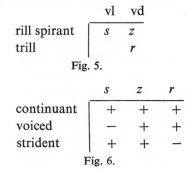

	vl	vd
rill spirant	*s*	*z*
trill		*r*

Fig. 5.

or,

	s	*z*	*r*
continuant	+	+	+
voiced	−	+	+
strident	+	+	−

Fig. 6.

or the like. Figure 5 shows a typical subsystem with the characteristic fault in symmetry resulting from imperfect utilization of all features (there is no distinctive voiceless *r* or trilled *s*). As a consequence the three can be arranged in a sequence such that with each step in either direction one feature specification in the matrix is changed,

$$s \longrightarrow z \longrightarrow r$$

Fig. 7.

while the relation is not to be pictured, for instance, as

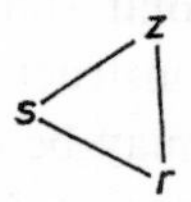

Fig. 8.

18.   Let it further be the case that the final stage, III, possesses wholly or in part the same subsystem *s z r*; that the phonological structure, in other words, has remained stable throughout. The neogrammarians, specialized as their area and period interests frequently were, would have accepted this as nothing more than what is to be expected.

19.   Now let the sound laws (replacements) operating within this stable subsystem and linking I with III be as follows: *s>r, z>r, r>r*; perhaps with further changes which recreate the disappearing entities *s* and *z* from other sources.[19]

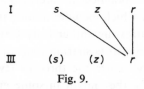

Fig. 9.

It is not likely that this state of affairs would be treated without some thought being given to the possibility or necessity of positing an intermediate state.

20.   Let us first consider the (minimal) replacement of *r* of stage I by *r* of stage III. It is fair to say that any interpretation under which the 'same' *r* were not to appear also at any intervening point in time would be regarded with suspicion.[20] Yet it is interesting that our knowledge, where it exists independently, sometimes causes us to recognize just such histories. The comparative method is powerful enough, and our records are full enough, to let us trace the German word for 'wind' through a series of ancestral stages most of which exhibit '*t*'-like and '*d*'-like sounds in fairly full contrast.

In the remote ancestor (IE) the word was something like *wĕntós* with *t*. In the Germanic subancestor Verner's law made the *t* into *d*, along with all other instances of *t* after an unaccented syllable other than after *s, p, k', kʷ*. In Old High German, all *d*'s went to *t*'s (the old slot being filled by *θ* going to '*d*'); this affected the *d* in the word for 'wind'. The records of later medieval German leave no doubt that all instances of *nt* (except before *r*) change to *nd*. In most forms of German, *d* apparently had its voicing at some time neutralized in syllable-final position in favor of *t*.[21] The dental in this word has thus consistently oscillated back and forth from *t* to *d* to *t* to *d* and (if the chronology is correct here) back to *t* (the modern High German shape is *vínt*). The case is not at all freakish but fully normal, and embedded in ordinary history. It also makes us remember that the stability of phonemic systems in the abstract is far from guaranteeing the inertness of the lexical materials existing in such a system.

21. To return to our model: the second 'change event' (since this is how the connecting lines in our scheme are likely to be labeled) is the replacement of *z* by *r*. If the question about plausible intermediate stages were asked here, it would have been answered for a long time by some reference to the assumed graduality of sound change. The rationale behind this assumption is not unlike that which is also responsible for the idea of the physically unchanged *r* just discussed. The passage of a *z*-like articulation to an *r*-like articulation of whatever variety was, and still is, pictured as a collective event which consists in the performance of a movement, occurrence by occurrence, from one articulation point or articulator shape to another, over time. There is a further inclination to think of this movement as traversing anatomically the shortest distance, at constant speed, during the period of transition between the two stable states. It is consistent with this picture to reckon with an infinite number of INTERMEDIATE STAGES for each of which articulation scatters around an intermediate point or shape of the articulatory apparatus. The assumed lack of motion in the earlier instance of *r > r* is a limiting case of the same thought.

22. Graduality has been discussed both speculatively and empirically. Some nineteenth-century scholars apparently thought that articulatory graduality is needed to explain the regularity of sound change – at least in the case of sound changes leading to a merger of contrast: if the changes were sudden, speakers would notice and 'correct' their behavior. It might be preferable to ask under what empirically known conditions sound substitution (Section 10), perhaps in small, one-feature sized but nevertheless distinct steps, takes place in such a way as to engulf all or most of the lexicon

– and hence to produce the picture of regular sound change. The empirical work is not yet conclusive.[22] Age grading in a population has sometimes been reported as articulatorily gradual[23]; but in large part it emerges instead as a matter of frequency of distinct performances: the incidence of one of two competing variants increases in inverse proportion to the speakers' age. Besides, the few follow-up studies in existence do not make it clear under what circumstances a finding of age grading has predictive value; i.e., when subjects, as they grow older persist in their own characteristic performance and when, contrariwise, they acquire the traits characteristic of more advanced age[24]. Many reports on ongoing mergers suggest an increase in the number of speakers who fail to observe an old contrast, but not a grad-ual phonetic weakening of it, and it is uncertain whether all of this is neces-sarily the fault of the observer who reacts in yes-or-no fashion only, even when he has phonetic training.[25] Lastly, as has often been said, some sound changes involve discontinuous articulators and have never been credibly described as proceeding either through intermediate positions or through a stage during which two articulations occur simultaneously.[26] In short, articulatory graduality is not a speculative necessity; and the typological outlandishness (say, simultaneous articulation as an intermediate stage in the change from *tí-tk-ō to Greek tíktō 'engender'; or from Latin factum 'done', coxa 'hip' to Rumanian fapt, coapsă) of some constructable inter-mediate stages makes general insistence on it unreasonable[27].

23.   To return to our model: there is no particular reality to the idea of discrete intermediate stages along the one-feature distance from z to r. This seems characteristically different when we examine the third replace-ment in III, namely the change from s to r. Here the distance to be tra-versed measures two, rather than the minimum one, distinctive features. On this basis alone the positing of an intermediate stage II is pronounced possi-ble. In harmony with the assumptions made earlier, s 'must' pass through z. The change from s to r proceeds in two distinct steps. The stability of phonological typology is preserved. Change, in this view, goes forward, not gradually, but by small steps, each one capable of being accommodated in a system of discrete points.[28] The picture is

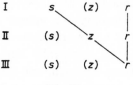

Fig. 10.

24. A further pleasing aspect on which comment exists and which, no doubt, plays a part in the acceptance of a proposed history, is the fact that here the succession of steps has direction: a succession $s>z>r$ can be interpreted, though perhaps only vaguely, as following a trend toward lenis articulation. As was pointed out before, a sequence $r>z>r$, even though it also involves two separate steps and also satisfies the preference for processes that do not require a modification of the framework, is thought less acceptable – the past of the dental stop in G *Wind* notwithstanding (Section 20).[29] Note also the overriding difference between the events of I/II and those of II/III. The latter lead to a merger (into r), while the former do not.

25. Our next task is to fit the history of the original z into the new three-stage picture, or to modify this picture, if necessary, in order to accommodate the old z. Here we first return for a moment to Figure 9 which represents the data for stages I and III before any relative chronological ordering. The picture has now been modified by inserting one intermediate stage (Figure 10) as required by the two-feature distance of $s>r$. However, Figure 9 has another weakness. Given a literal chronological interpretation, it would seem to signify not one merger but two simultaneous mergers with one and the same outcome at stage III. Since the presence of a merger is rightly regarded as the strongest argument for positing a stage, this is important.[30] One comment might be that physical simultaneity is too extreme an accident to be plausible. As the problem is really one of ordering alleged change events, a clearer way of expressing it is to ask whether those two mergers must remain unordered or whether it is possible to show that either of two orderings is preferable – always assuming that each merger process is indeed a well-defined whole. In other words: is it possible to say that z was first merged with r (into z or into r?), with the product, in turn, merging with s into r? Or was z first merged with s (into z or into s?), with a subsequent merger of the product with r? Either way, the old constraints are heeded: an available, stable, one-feature-at-a-time subsystem s–z–r, and displacement to the extent of one feature per stage interval.

26. One conceivable solution is, then,

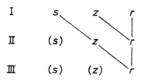

Fig. 11.

The history in question is accommodated within the three stages that are needed in any event because of the distance which one factor, the original s, has to traverse. There is, however, a consequence which has troubled some observers, though not those who think in purely Saussurian terms; the changes $s > z$ and $z > r$, while they do not have the same target, still appear as taking place 'simultaneously', or in unordered fashion. The literature contains some implicit doubts about the nature of this simultaneity. It is as though a minimum stage interval ought not only to limit its welcome to displacements of minimum (one-feature) magnitude, but also to a minimum number (one) of such displacements.

27.   If these hesitations are taken seriously, the following way out might be followed:

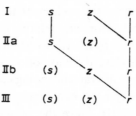

Fig. 12.

The array is familiar to those who address themselves to the causation of change events. Since s cannot go to z before a void has been created at z (or it would 'feed' the z which goes to r),[31] and since simultaneity is suspect, s is declared to go to z 'after' z goes to r, for the 'purpose', or at least with the effect, of restoring stability to a temporarily perturbed system.[32] In sum, if only the minimum number of minimum displacements is allowed per stage interval, the tendency would be to recognize two intermediate stages IIa and IIb rather than only one.

28.   But what if the binary mergers required (Section 25) are arranged in descending order of the magnitude (measured in one-feature steps) of the distance which each phoneme (of stage I) must traverse in order to reach its goal (at stage III)? For the old s this distance is 2, for z it is 1, and for r it is 0, thus

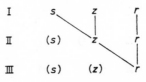

Fig. 13.

This, then, figures as the optimum solution. It avoids more-than-minimum movements per interval; it avoids simultaneity of displacements as well as simultaneity of mergers; and it allows the two stages II and III to be defined in the clearest possible way, namely through mergers. At the same time it operates with an economic minimum of stages.

30.   The preceding example, with its various solutions involves so-called unconditional change.[33] When this is not the case, the problem may be more complex but it may also be richer in elements to favor particular, less arbitrary solutions. Consider the following. The environments in which s z r occur will be subdivided uniformly (complete uniformity being specified here for simplicity's sake only; the construction could be made more general). In environment 1 (say, after pause before a vowel) $s > z, z > z, r > r$. In environment 2 (say, between vowels) all three items end up as r, as heretofore.

In environment 1 (·····):

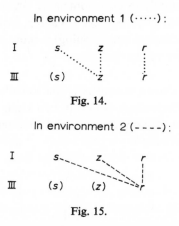

Fig. 14.

In environment 2 (- - - -):

Fig. 15.

Let now the 'optimum' solution (Figure 13) be adopted for the environment class 2, for the reasons stated above. The question is then asked what chronological relation the developments in environment 1 bear to those in 2. If it is thought that there is no systematic relation at all it will clearly be necessary, in order to avoid simultaneity of displacements, to multiply the number of stages. If we do wish to establish some relationship, we might first try

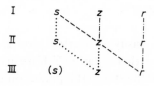

Fig. 16.

with the result, possibly objectionable, of producing such simultaneity. If we choose this alternative,

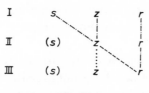

Fig. 17.

we have a solution which carries strong conviction. It may be said that, at stage II, *s* has changed unconditionally (and merged with *z*, likewise unconditionally). The first merger product of the 'optimum' solution (Section 29) then survives separately in environment 1. Or, to put it differently, the splitting up of what used to be, at stage I, *s* and *z*, along the same allophonic dividing lines (under identical conditioning) is more economically explained as having occurred once rather than twice.

31.   One of the best known examples is the so-called vowel weakening of Latin which in part affects short vowels in two kinds of word-interior syllables, open or ending in the vowel (————) and checked or ending in a consonant (. . . . .).

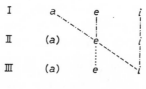

Fig. 18.

Examples are: *cōnfaciō* > (*cōnfeciō* >) *cōnficiō* 'accomplish'; *cōnfactus* > > *cōnfectus* 'accomplished'; *conteneō* > *contineō* 'hold together'; *contentus* (from a still earlier *-ņ-*) > *contentus* 'satisfied'; *aditus* > *aditus* 'access'; *magister* > *magister* 'master'.[34]

32.   This reasoning is easily converted into a formulation of relative chronology made on an earlier occasion.[35] If we arrange our stage I alphabet on one axis of a grid and the stage III alphabet on the other, and note, in the appropriate cell, in which environment classes the stage-III replacements

occur, we obtain

I	s	z	r	III
				(s)
	1	1		z
	2	2	1 2	r

Fig. 19.

where we note the recurrence of the same environment label ('1', '2') in each
of the two lines ('z', 'r') as these intersect with the same columns ('s', 'z').[36]
The prescription for interpreting this 'square pattern' is to state that s was
merged with z under conditions 1 and 2, and that the merger product 'S'
subsequently split, once only, into z (in environment 1) and r (in environment 2):

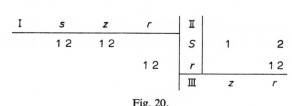

Fig. 20.

33.   The processes here described exemplify in large measure the chronological counterpart of an additive or 'feeding' rule order: the merger at the
intermediate stage adds to the lexical material which is headed for the
second change at the final stage, as the obvious geometry of the arrays shows.
Is there a converse subtractive, 'bleeding' chronology? In a sense there is,
though it is of necessity a negative affair. It is vaguer and more vulnerable
because the recognition of two elements from different stages as being the
same may rest on the validity of particular notations. Consider Figures 13
and 11. The question there was, in effect, whether $s>z$ is in a feeding or in
a bleeding relationship with regard to $z>r$; whether the merger of the old
s with the old z did occur or did not occur ('was avoided') at the second stage
(disregarding for the moment the second interval leading to the third stage).
It turned out that choice of the bleeding relationship could prove costly in
that it might lead to the positing of an additional intermediate stage. Many
of the histories involving 'drag chain' mechanisms or the horror vacui (of
the cases vides) belong here. In fact, stage IIa in Figure 12 exhibits precisely
the gap at z, a gap which presumably constitutes a typological anomaly to be
remedied in the subsequent development. The 'push-chain' mechanism, if
an effort were made to fit it into[37] a diachronic framework would, in part,

look somewhat like this:

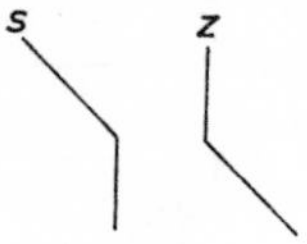

Fig. 21.

the anomaly in this case consisting not in a gap but in the need for a new position, to the right of *s*, in the framework. It may of course be the case, empirically, that the most faithful representation of the behavior of parts of the speaking population is the one suggested by Figure 11 with its implication of graduality coupled with a permanency of the distances kept by the contrasting items. This would apply to non-merging, 'shift' processes so typical for vowels and for certain types of consonant subsystems.

34.   Once again the history of the treatment of the Germanic consonants furnishes a familiar example. Some scholars see Grimm's law necessarily as a bleeding complex:

$$t > \theta$$
$$d > t$$
$$\text{'}dh\text{'} > d$$

Fig. 22.

or,

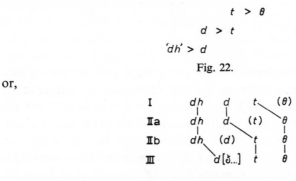

Fig. 23.

either in intermediate stages with cases vides first at *t* and then at *d* (Figure 23) or in terms of continuous movement. Others, partly on grounds of outside evidence in the guise of loanwords, propose other sequences and, in particular, have *d>t* follow after *dh>d*.[38] Since, however, *dh>d* does not feed into *d>t*, recourse is had to the argument that IE *d* and Gc *d* were presumably phonetically apart, IE *d* being a stop and Germanic *d* (in many of its allophones) apparently a non-strident spirant [đ]. Some would interpret this in the push-chain sense.

35.   There is a somewhat different special case of subtractive relationship which is more nearly the converse of the additive sequences studied earlier.

Those sequences were meant to exemplify the case in which our historical grammars describe two or more merger processes converging toward one and the same target ('*r*'). When these merger processes are accompanied by split processes, with the residues staying behind unmerged, this traditionally suggests inferences, which, when open to control, turn out to be fairly close to factual history. On the whole, merger processes and their target-sharing pattern constitute unmistakable hard facts which no difference in notation can obscure. Now, changes, including merger processes, may also, in a much weaker sense of the statement, share their starting point rather than their endpoint. This is the case when the starting point consists of phones assigned to one and the same phonemic unit under a specific chosen notation. Thus voiceless proto-Greek stops (dental, labiovelar, labial) moved as follows in Attic:

Fig. 24.

k^w before front vowels (–––––) merging with *t*, otherwise in most environments (.....) merging with *p*. These processes are in a quasi-subtractive relationship which is mutual. By going to *t* the front allophone of k^w 'escapes' a hypothetical unconditional[39] change to *p*, and the same is true, mutatis mutandis, for the back allophone going to *p*. Clearly, in view of the symmetry of the situation there are no strong formal arguments for preferring the sequence

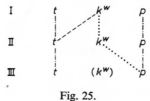

Fig. 25.

to the sequence

Fig. 26.

Both avoid the possibly unpleasing simultaneity of two merger events (Section 30). One of the two may, however, well happen to create a typologically more acceptable immediate stage than the other.[40] In grid form (Section 32) this configuration is likewise characteristic:

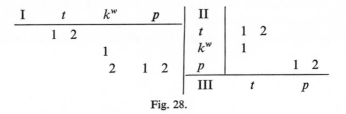

Fig. 27.

where the solution corresponding to that of Figure 26 is

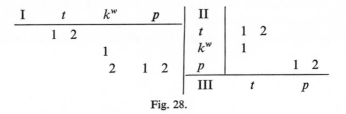

Fig. 28.

36.   In German there are two rules, and two sound changes, which can affect a syllable final *ng*, as in *láng* 'long'. One devoices *g* in syllable-final position; the other deletes *g* after *n* [ŋ]. In some dialects the outcome is *láŋk*: (dotted = 'at syllable end'; broken = 'not at syllable end'; heavy = 'after [ŋ]'; light = 'not after [ŋ]'):

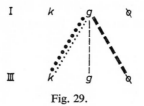

Fig. 29.

in other dialects, it is *láŋ*:

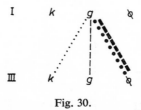

Fig. 30.

If *láŋk*, the devoicing has removed potential material from the deletion rule; if *láŋ*, the deletion has removed potential material from the devoicing rule. Consequently, the case has been called one of 'mutual bleeding'.[41] The historian might interpret it thus for *láŋk* (Figure 29):

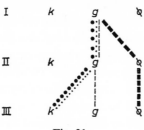

Fig. 31.

or:

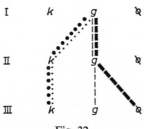

Fig. 32.

and thus for *láŋ* (Figure 30):

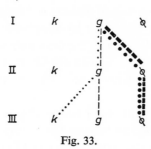

Fig. 33.

or:

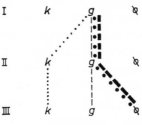

Fig. 34.

so long as he simply overlays the array for $g > k$ with that for $g > \varnothing$. But when the two are really considered together, a degree of superiority of Figures 32 and 33 over Figures 31 and 34 becomes evident. It lies in the fact that the split processes are more plausibly conditioned in Figures 32 and 33. A form like *lánge* is characterized by having its *g* occur (1) after *n*, and (2) not at syllable end. There would be nothing remarkable in *lánge* splitting off and losing its *g* first (Figure 31), if *láng árg* 'bad' *árge* were to remain phonologically united, by either retaining or devoicing their *g* without distinction. But the circumstance that one component in the conditioning – namely, the matter of syllable end – has to apply a second time at the intermediate stage is displeasing. The same is true, mutatis mutandis, for Figure 34. The split processes described in Figures 32 and 33 reflect, on the other hand, one rule each.

37.   It remains to examine briefly the use of certain other kinds of simplicity argument. Some sound changes, when viewed from initial to final stage, are under a given notation unconditional. Other sound changes are conditioned in ways which are still relatively simple to state and follow some natural, perhaps assimilatory, principle or have a concrete and clearly visible typological direction. It seems that many sound changes are at first tied to a narrow conditioning which then continues to widen. In the simplest case, that is, when (among other factors) the notation happens to be fully congenial to the history in question, the change works itself out to non-conditioned status. In many Greek dialects *w* disappears 'gradually' that is, position after position, or allophone by allophone: first after some consonants, then between vowels, then at the beginning of words before a vowel (the merger being mostly 'with ⊘'). In the Greek which has survived antiquity the loss of *w* is, as the matter is customarily put, complete.[42]

38.   If context-free (unconditioned) sound changes are intrinsically 'simpler', as some theorists seem to believe, the history just described gains in, or tends to, simplicity as it traverses a number of more complex states. The same may perhaps also be granted where the target is not marked by complete absence of conditioning under the notation chosen, but rather in the following manner. Some Algonquian languages have lost their final vowels, thereby creating a well-defined, outstanding canonic shape for words; these all end in consonants, though there is a larger variety of final consonants and consonant clusters than there were vowel finals at the previous stage.[43] It would be absurd to expect this kind of conditioned change to move on past the typological optimum toward an unconditioned status through which all vowels everywhere would be lost. As a characteristic of direction in sound change the principle of widening conditioning is therefore not absolute, although within certain typologically set limits this variety of directionality through 'small steps' does appear to operate.

39.   Our study of the role of conditioned merger in the setting up of intermediate stages indicates that intermediate-stage problems are often posed
as though they were merely questions about the succession in time of sound
changes already given as separate entities (Section 30). It is indeed quite
easy to pick out the two one-feature (hence plausible) alterations which
figure overtly in a comparison of the initial with the final stage ($s>z$, $z>r$),
and to note their complementary character

Fig. 35.

and the further fact that there is a second pair which consists of one no-feature
and one two-feature alteration:

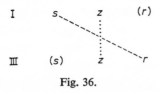

Fig. 36.

The two-feature alteration demands an intermediate stage, and the two
known one-feature changes first observed are interpreted as

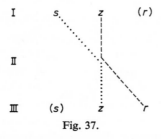

Fig. 37.

so as to fit them in with Figure 36 into the composite pattern of Figure 17.

40.   Let us now consider the properties of a case which is classical. In a
perfunctory way W. Porzig, for one, mentions, as self-evident, the conclusion
that the change $sr>str$ in Slavic must be more recent than the change $k'>s$
since $sr<k'r$ goes to str as well.[44] Now, the contrastive core of the case lies
in the fact that IE $k'r$, sr, and str all end up as merged, into str, in Slavic.

This may be represented thus (– – – – = 'before *r*'):

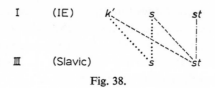

Fig. 38.

hence, by starting with this skeleton (compare Figure 36)

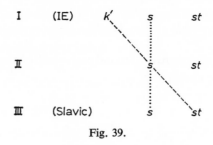

Fig. 39.

and, going through the motions analogous to those of Figure 37, as

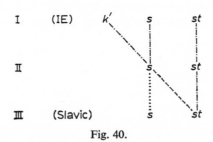

Fig. 40.

Note, however, that phonetic directionality is not overly pronounced. It would be arbitrary to see a physical progression in the sequence *k'–s–st*. On the other hand, since contrast between *s* and *st* (that is, between ⊗ and *t*) does not exist before *r* (after *s*, before *r*) at the final stage, it is not arbitrary to seize upon such phonetic differences (of 'release' etc.) as make *st* in general (e.g. before vowel) and [sᵗ] before *r* – where [ᵗ] may be labeled automatic – unlike each other, and to write the [sᵗr] of the final stage as /sr/ with an automatic subphonemic glide.[45] In this case there is nothing to prevent positing the following chronological sequence

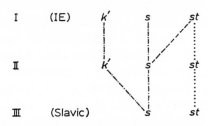

Fig. 41.

in which *sr* and *str* merge first, while *k'* and *s* (including, if one wishes, *k'r* and *sr* respectively) are still distinct. The point is that the change affecting *k'* is not so obviously a two-feature affair under these conditions (Section 23). Quite systematic-sounding rationalizations lie ready to hand: first *sr* and *str* merge into [sʲr]; then *k'* merges with [s] 'wherever [s] occurs', and with [sʲ] wherever [s] does not occur. Note that the feeding relationship remains intact in both arrays.

41. It is true, however, that in this particular instance system stability asserts itself in the end. What is missing at stage III – temporarily, it turns out – is after all not *st* but *sr*, since much later, under a chronology of which we have direct as well as 'comparatively' reconstructed knowledge, *sr* ... is created anew (from *serC*, *sorC* in several Slavic languages; from Slavic *sъr*, etc.).[46]

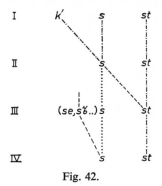

Fig. 42.

Clearly, the old (*sr*, *k'r*>) *sr*>*str* stands in a bleeding relationship to *ser*, *sor*, *sъr*>*sr*. ...

41. What one learns from these and many other examples is the subtlety and precariousness of relationships which on the surface appear to have immediate cogency. It is quite likely that many particular classical interpreta-

tions involving intermediate stages and relative chronologies are in fact accurate. This does not alter the desirability of further formalizing some of their aspects. In general, bleeding relationships, in themselves rather weak of formulation since this formulation depends on judgments about 'identities' from stage to stage, are nevertheless worth recognizing. The chronological sequence in a bleeding relationship can sometimes be reversed only at the cost of denying such identities, and at the cost of synchronic proliferation of structure points without typological plausibility. Feeding relationships are irreducible as such. The preferred order of the steps seems to be that which allows a minimum number of minimum (one-feature) steps per stage, but no accidents of simultaneity, especially of multiple, simultaneous merger. Where these factors are doubtful, the relative chronologies themselves may collapse, though not to the point where the additive or subtractive nature of a complex of changes is called into doubt (see Note 31).

CHAPTER II

THE THREE-WITNESS PROBLEM

1. The use of the model of the rooted tree in many phases of linguistics needs no introductory comment. Its most anciently familiar form is the family tree in which so-called lines of descent are represented by edges and paths, languages (given or reconstructed) by vertices, subancestor languages by nodes or vertices of local degree greater than two, the overall ancestor by the root, and the passage of time by direction away from the root.[47] In the history of scholarship the setting up of family trees may have drawn inspiration from analogous uses of tree models in other fields of knowledge, notably from the evolutionary tree with its 'lines of descent' and from the manuscript stemma used by students of written and printed texts to show the dependency (by copying, etc.) of one witness from another. For reasons of historical accident, as well as for intrinsic ones, it is the last-mentioned influence in particular which has been at work, and which has turned out to be fruitful.

2. A number of languages descended separately from one ancestor (a number of manuscripts copied from one model[48]) may be expected to share innovations (common errors) of a non-trivial sort only by accident. If accident can be excluded and if innovations (errors) can be independently recognized as such, subancestors (hyparchetypes) and the ancestor (archetype) may be reconstructed and the resulting tree may be historically interpreted in terms of separation, migration, etc. (in terms of monastic history, of the history of writing and printing, etc.).

3. One of the chief premises, in this view, is that of the recognizability of innovation (error). As for manuscript error, there has been skepticism:[49] since the choices of expression available to writers of the past are never known except through the very texts that are being studied, the decision is circular; errors have been suspected in cases where independent evidence has confirmed the 'anomaly' as a mere 'singularity'; and so on.[50] Some are not even willing to recognize misspellings resulting in palpably meaningless jumbles as errors in this sense. There, classical scholars have been in a somewhat more favorable position than, for instance, Anglists in that classicists sometimes deal with altogether mechanical types of tradition in which even gross mistakes will survive. Still, there has been a search for techniques which would make it possible to circumvent decisions on what constitutes error.

4.   For language family trees this is precisely different. In scholarly practice (though not always in stated theory) trees depend more heavily on phonological than on any other kind of evidence. The fact that once a tree is known it can be enriched with non-phonological data of far greater importance does not alter this position. There are good reasons for it. The 'comparative' method (Section 39) in the narrower sense of this term functions by itself as a discovery procedure to distinguish phonological innovation from phonological retention of a certain kind.[51] The innovations and retentions in question have to do with the existence and destruction of contrast.[52] If a in language A sometimes matches m, and at other times (in other morphs, that is) n, in language B, in the same phonological surroundings, the contrast is old ($x > a$, $y > a$, with 'merger' in A; $x > m$, $y > n$ with retention of the distinction in B). If the surroundings of the two correspondences a/m, a/n are complementary, the contrast is the result of a change ($x > a$ in A; $x_{\text{environment 1}} > m$, $x_{\text{environment 2}} > n$ in B) in which A has not participated. In Sanskrit, k, c are the result of a split when compared with Lithuanian k, k. Skt. c corresponds to Lith. k when these sounds precede a Skt. a which corresponds to a Lith. e, a Skt. i corresponding to a Lith. i, etc.; but a Skt. k corresponds to a Lith. k before a Skt. and Lith. a, a Skt. and Lith. r, etc. In theory, when the construction of language family trees is problematic, it is not for reasons analogous to those put forward by the skeptics who merely question the recognizability of textual innovation.

5.   As in the case of manuscripts (granting that some errors can be recognized as such) the matching, called 'comparison', of two languages may have one of two kinds of result. Either, one contains all the innovations, or each contains at least one. In the first case the reconstruction collapses with one of the two given languages (say, A) which is then 'like' the ancestor of the other (B). Since it is known that all language changes, the conclusion is that A 'is' the ancestor of B and may be predicted to precede B in real time. In the second case there are two lines of descent from the ancestor, X, each one carrying the respective innovation(s) along with retentions (see Chapter I, Section 12).

6.   Let us consider some properties of language family trees accommodating a number of given related languages, A, B, C, ...). It is useful to distinguish three kinds of vertices: (1) L-points (marked ∘) each of which represents one of the languages that are given; if the vertices are terminal, they represent languages without descendants, or languages here considered without their descendants. (2) Nodes, i.e. points of local degree three or greater, representing reconstructable subancestors (labeled Y, or numbered 1, 2, 3 ...)

dominating more than one immediate descendant, either given or reconstructed; nodes are L's, L's are nodes when given languages, upon application of
the comparative method, turn out to be subancestors. (3) The root point,
X, representing the overall ancestor; again, X, may be an L-point or a node
or both, or (most generally) neither. It is sometimes helpful to consider a
language family tree as non-rooted, though with all its other properties intact.

7.   Examples are:

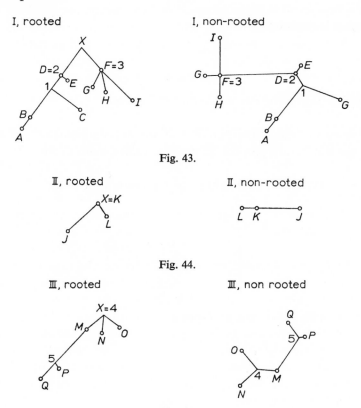

Fig. 43.

Fig. 44.

Fig. 45.

8.   THREE given languages may form two non-rooted trees. First, there is

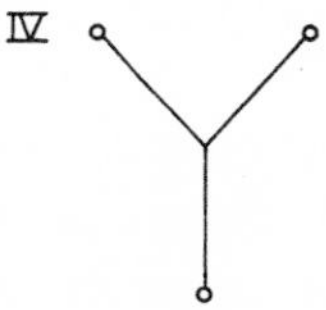

Fig. 46.

with all *L*-points terminal and one triple node. Second, if one of the *L*-points is moved into the node so as to eliminate one edge,

Fig. 47.

we obtain II (see above)

Fig. 48.

with two terminal and one non-terminal *L*-point.

9.   For each of these, insertion of *X* at any of the topologically distinctive locations will in turn produce all possible rooted trees, to wit:

IVa   *X* is neither an *L*-point nor the node

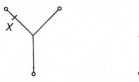

Fig. 49.

IVb   *X* is an *L*-point

Fig. 50.

IVc   *X* is the node

Fig. 51.

IIa   *X* is not an *L*-point

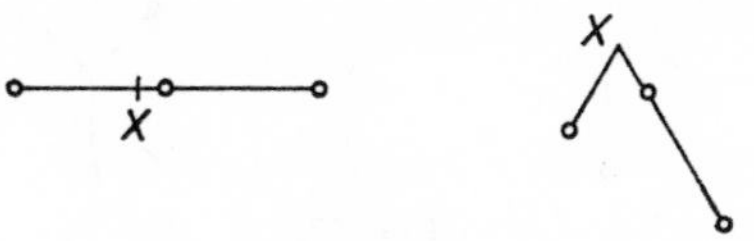

Fig. 52.

IIb   *X* is one of the terminal *L*-points

Fig. 53.

IIc   *X* is the non-terminal *L*-point

Fig. 54.

10.   Since the given languages *A*, *B*, and *C* may be distributed as follows among the two trees in their non-rooted forms:

IV   one distribution

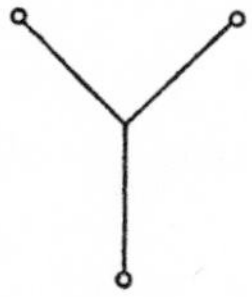

Fig. 55.

II   three distributions

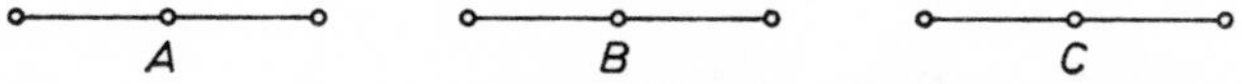

Fig. 56.

the following distributions exist as the root point is inserted:

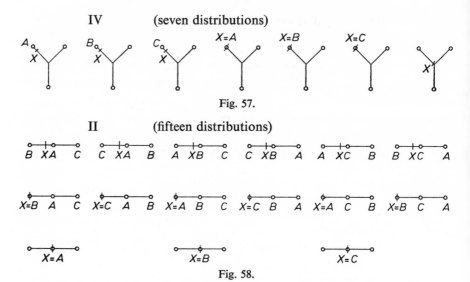

Fig. 57.

Fig. 58.

Thus, when given in their conventional form (with *X* at the top of the diagram), the following twenty-two rooted trees exist for *A*, *B*, and *C*:[53]

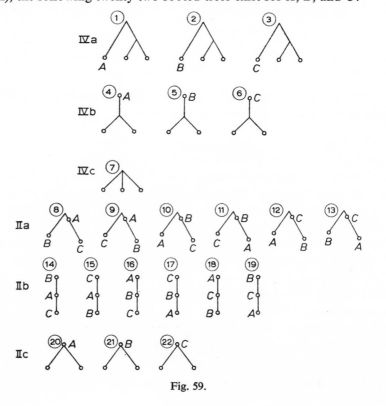

Fig. 59.

11.   An important line of thought was developed, in the course of manuscript (not language) work, by Dom Quentin 'who made a determined effort to avoid treating readings as right and wrong and to study them all equally as variants'.[54] Quentin's central concept is that of the 'intermediary' – a witness *B* (a manuscript or print) out of three, *A*, *B*, *C*, such that there are readings of *A* and *B* against *C*, of *C* and *B* against *A*, but none of *A* and *C* against *B*. This places some limitations on possible stemmata (trees). Some otherwise possible trees from our table (Figure 59) can be eliminated without any knowledge of textual right or wrong. Let us consider why this is so.

12.   *A*, *B*, and *C* exhibit the following classes of readings: in certain places of the text

> *A* reads *d*,
> *B* reads *d*,
> *C* reads *e*,

while in others

> *A* reads *f*,
> *B* reads *g*,
> *C* reads *g*.[55]

The fact that in the majority of cases all manuscripts read *k*, *k*, *k* may be disregarded. The combination *l*, *m*, *l* is of course specifically excluded by the construction of the problem. Individual readings, *i*, *j*, *h*, have only limited interest.[56]

13.   Let us start with the tree shape IIa, and let us assume that the three manuscripts are related as under nos. 8, 9 (Figure 59). No matter which reading the archetype *X* has, the descendant of *A* would have had to duplicate the *g* of the other branch by accidentally duplicating, or accidentally reversing, a change (a factor which it is in theory possible to guard against with statistical means). The same is true mutatis mutandis for nos. 12 and 13; here the reading *d d e* (in *A B C*, respectively) is incompatible with a history where *C*, with its special reading, intervenes between *X* and its own dependent.

14.   In nos. 14, 15 (tree IIb), *A* is a (known) intermediate stage between *B* and *C*, and between *C* and *B*; in nos. 18, 19 the same is true of *C* with regard to *A* and *B*, and *B* and *A*. But *B* and *C* share the reading *g* against the *f* of *A*, and *A* and *B* share *d* against the *e* of *C*, so that in all these cases the later copy would have had to reverse the copying error or change of the intermediate copy.

15.   Again, in the case of IIc: in no. 20 (22), if A (C) is the archetype and both dependents share a reading g (d) against the original f (e), the dependents, if truly separate, must have accidentally duplicated each other's deviation.

16.   No tree IV (noded) will accommodate an intermediary. This is true not only for no. 7 (IVc) where it is obvious that no one dependent holds a privileged position such as the intermediary must; it is just as true for IVa, b, where the specially related dependents – say, B and C in nos. 1, 4, or A and C in nos. 2, 5 – may very well share readings against the third, privileged dependent. These readings are then hyparchetypal (see below, Section 27).

17.   What Quentin's term thus expresses is the fact that the limitation on stemmata to accommodate an 'intermediary' is controlled by their non-rooted shape: the trees (non-noded) underlain by

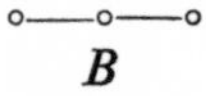

$$\circ\!\!-\!\!\!-\!\!\circ\!\!-\!\!\!-\!\!\circ$$
$$B$$

Fig. 60.

(where B is the intermediary), and only those trees, will do so. To put it somewhat differently, if A shares no readings with C against B, either A, or C, is a copy of B. The other of the two (C, or A) is either another copy (no. 21) or the model (nos. 16, 17) of B, or (nos. 10, 11) shares its model, X, with B.

18.   In noded (IV) and non-noded (II) trees (stemmata) alike it is in part possible to classify features (readings), shared as well as unshared, into innovations (deviations, results of 'change') and retentions. For instance, readings $k\,k\,k$ shared by three manuscripts $A\,B\,C$ are retentions, since independent twofold (IVa) or even threefold (IVc) occurrence of one and the same innovation is to be excluded as improbable.

19.   IVb, IIb, and IIc are open to inspection inasmuch as in these stemmata the archetype is one of the known manuscripts. Thus, in IVb (no. 5), given the following classes of readings (in addition to $k\,k\,k$):

A reads d, and			A reads f, while		
B	d, but	and	B	g, and	
C	e;		C	g,	

as before, but also (as is proper in a noded tree):

A reads l,	
B	m,
C	l,

It is clear that the readings which the archetype B shares with A against C (namely, d) and with C against A (namely, g) are retentions, that the readings shared by A and C (namely, l) are innovations of the hyparchetype, and that e and f are particular innovations of C and of A, respectively. Consequently, there is a RELATIVE CHRONOLOGY: in terms of the archetype, m is replaced earlier; d and g, where they are not retained, are replaced later. The hyparchetype contains all the majority readings, $*d$ $*g$ (retained) and $*l$ (innovated) ($* =$ 'reconstructed').

20.   In the non-noded stemmata IIb (say, 16) and IIc (say, 21) l m l is absent. In No. 16, g is innovated in B at the first or intermediate stage, and e is innovated in C at the final stage. Again the hyparchetype, that is the intermediate stage, contains the two shared readings, one retained (d), one innovated (g). In no. 21 the archetype is the Quentin intermediary with d, g; A replaces g with f, while C replaces d with e.

21.   The types IVa, IVc, and IIa in which not only the hyparchetypes but also the archetypes need to be reconstructed, rather than merely inspected, offer greater interest. In IVa (no. 2), with sharing patterns as above (Section 19) the separately descended manuscript B shares d and g with each of the hyparchetypally descended A and C, respectively, against the other, while A and C, in turn, share l against B. Once more, the hyparchetype Y (the model of A and C) reads the majority variants, $*d$ $*g$ $*l$: the first two because they occur in B as well, so that their reappearance, through innovation, in either dependent of Y would have to be a matter of accidental reversion to a lost stage, and l because, if it were not in Y it would have had to be introduced into each dependent by a duplication of the same replacement process. As for the archetype X, it must have $*g$ $*d$ for the reasons indicated; but whether it has $*l$ or $*m$, that is, whether m is a particular innovation of the separate dependent B, or l is an innovation of the hyparchetype cannot be decided. In this defined sense the archetype is only PARTIALLY RECONSTRUCTABLE.

22.   In IVc (no. 7) the node is the archetype; it may be said that archetype and hyparchetype coincide. We are therefore not surprised to see that all the shared readings (d g l) are retentions from the archetype. They have to be, because as innovations they would have to reflect a duplication in two of the three separate dependents.

23.   IIa – say, no. 10 – is non-noded and thus lacks the class l m l. The relation between the intermediary (and intermediate) B and its dependent C is clear: C's e is innovated, and its g is retained, from its model B. The arche-

type, X, has *d (if it had *e like C but unlike B, we would be dealing with an accidental reversion); but whether it has *f (like A) or *g (like B) cannot be known in any given case. X is only partially reconstructable.

24.   In sum,

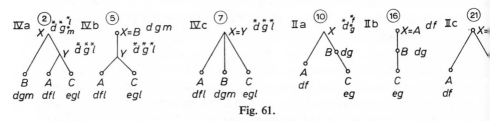

Fig. 61.

25.   So far we have disregarded all independent qualitative knowledge of what constitutes innovation, what retention. In the field of manuscript study this attitude is sometimes considered a source of strength (see Section 3 above). Even there, however, it may be the case that of two competing variants (such as, for example, particular instances subsumed under d vs. e in our constructions) one is clearly an 'error' while the other is acceptable. Unless the acceptable variant can have arisen by conjecture, the chances are, then, that the source possessed it and that the 'error' is a deviation from the source. It is important that nothing stronger than this is needed to yield certain important results. Neither is it necessary, for the purpose under consideration, to be able to choose between two variants both of which are 'acceptable', nor that ALL the particular variants subsumed under a sharing pattern of the kind that we have been considering be classified with regard to 'error'. Rather, it is possible to find the appropriate tree for three witnesses A B C if SOME variants can be identified as 'errors'. The procedure may be outlined as follows.

26.   In keeping with what has been said before, passages of the text extant in A B C will fall into these three, or four, significant classes, namely

(α)	those in which all three witnesses agree	k k k
(β)	those in which A and B have one variant and C has another	d d e
(γ)	those in which B and C have one variant and A has another	f g g
	and, in some instances but not in others,	
(δ)	those in which A and C have one variant and B has another	l m l

27.   If (α), (β), (γ) and (δ) are present, the tree is noded (IV). If only (α), (β) and (γ) are present, the tree is non-noded.

If the classes d g l do not include cases of 'error' and e f m do, the stemma is IVc (no. 7), and ALL instances of *d g l* are archetypal (retained). Conversely, ALL instances of *e f m* are 'errors' (innovated), the deviations having occurred separately in *A*, *B*, or *C*. See above, Section 22.

If the classes *e f l* contain 'errors' and *d g m* do not, the stemma is IVb, with *B* as the archetype. The hyparchetype *Y* has *d *g *l. ALL instances of *e f l* are 'errors' (innovations). See above, Section 19.

If both *l* and *m* include 'errors' – in other words, if *A* and *C* share some 'errors' against *B*, while, in other passages, *B* shows an 'error' against a joint reading of *A* and *C* – and *e* and *f* do, too, the stemma is IVa, with *B* in the privileged position of the separate dependent (no. 2). ALL cases of *d* and *g* are retentions; ALL cases of *e f* are innovations (in terms of the archetype); in instances where *m* is an 'error', *l* is archetypal, and where *l* is an 'error', *m* is archetypal. In other words, the archetype has *d *g and in some passages *l, in others *m, and is not reconstructable as between the two in a third group of passages, where no 'error' was recognized in either witness. The hyparchetype *Y* has *d *g *l, where some instances of *l are retained and others are innovated. See above, Section 21.

28.   If (δ) is absent from the data, the tree is non-noded (II), with *B* as a Quentin intermediary.

If *d g* do not include 'errors', while *e f* do, the stemma is IIc (no. 21), with *B* as the ancestor. ALL examples of *d g* are archetypal and retained, whereas ALL examples of *e f* are innovated. See above, Section 19.

If *g e* include 'errors' and *d f* do not, the stemma is IIb, with *A* as the archetype and *B* as an extant intermediate stage. *B* has introduced ALL instances of *g* (to replace *f*), *C* has introduced ALL instances of *e* (to replace *d*) See above, Section 19.

If *g f* both include 'errors', and *e* does, too, the stemma is II a (no. 10). All instances of *e* are innovations. The archetype *X* has *d in ALL cases; it has *f in some passages and *g in others. See above, Section 22.

29.   For a summary in tabular form, SEE FIGURE 62 ON THE NEXT PAGE, and note that where *X*, in addition to having to be identified (IVb, IIb, IIc), needs to be reconstructed (IVa, IVc, IIa), this can be done fully for IVc, and partially for IVa and IIa.[57] *Y* is always fully reconstructable.

30.   In addition to the distribution of variants among the witnesses (Sections 11–24) and to the intrinsic claim of variants to relative originality (Sections 25–29), the chronological order in which manuscripts were written may happen to be known. This is of importance because a line of descent in a stemma also represents an ordering in time. In general, of course, archetypes

If classes of variants shared by

A and B//against C	B and C//against A	A and C//against B	the trees are:

contain known 'errors' as follows:

A and B//against C	B and C//against A	A and C//against B	
----//'errors'	----//'errors'	'errors'//'errors'	IVa (2)
----//'errors'	----//'errors'	'errors'//----	IVb (5)
----//'errors'	----//'errors'	----//'errors'	IVc (7)
----//'errors'	'errors'//'errors'		IIa (10)
----//'errors'	'errors'//----		IIb (16)
----//'errors'	----//'errors'		IIc (21)

Fig. 62.

antedate hyparchetypes and other manuscripts. In particular, and with regard to the L-points of the stemmata, the types IVa and IVc, with no linkage of L-points by lines of descent, will fit any relative ordering of writing (copying) dates for A, B, C; if lines of descent are drawn to different vertical distances from X to indicate (metrically) real time, we may for instance have

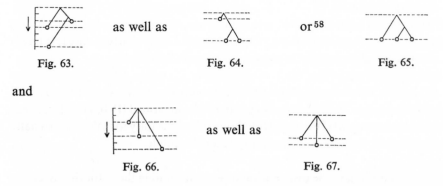

Fig. 63.   as well as   Fig. 64.   or [58]   Fig. 65.

and

Fig. 66.   as well as   Fig. 67.

The other types do, however, impose restrictions. A given IVb stemma allows two orderings inasmuch as the witness functioning as archetype must antedate the others. Thus, no. 5 allows $B \rightarrowtail A \rightarrowtail C$[59] and $B \rightarrowtail C \rightarrowtail A$ (as well as simultaneity of A and C).

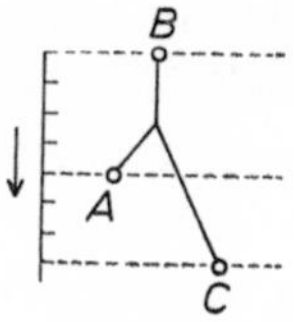

Fig. 68. 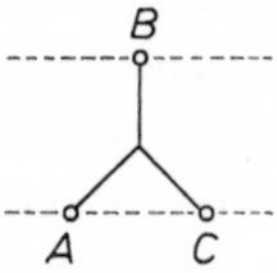   Fig. 69.

The same obviously holds for IIc; a given such stemma, say, no. 21, allows the same two orderings, $B \rightarrowtail A \rightarrowtail C$ and $B \rightarrowtail C \rightarrowtail A$. In IIa two witnesses are on one line of descent (in no. 10, B and C), while the third (in no. 10, A) is separate. As a result, a given tree, say no. 10, allows three chronological orderings, $A \rightarrowtail B \rightarrowtail C$, $B \rightarrowtail A \rightarrowtail C$, and $B \rightarrowtail C \rightarrowtail A$ (and also simultaneity of A and B or A and C, but not of B and C). In the case of IIb each stemma allows one ordering only (in no. 16, $A \rightarrowtail B \rightarrowtail C$) and no simultaneity.

For any one Quentin intermediary (say B) each of those two triple orderings in which the intermediary has the earliest date ($B \rightarrowtail A \rightarrowtail C$, $B \rightarrowtail C \rightarrowtail A$) is compatible with two IIa stemmata (nos. 10, 11) and with one IIc stemma (no. 21); each of those two triple orderings in which the intermediary is second in time ($A \rightarrowtail B \rightarrowtail C$, $C \rightarrowtail B \rightarrowtail A$) is compatible with one IIa (nos. 10 or 11, respectively) and one IIb (nos. 16 or 17, respectively) stemma, while the two orderings with the intermediary in the most recent location ($A \rightarrowtail C \rightarrowtail B$, $C \rightarrowtail A \rightarrowtail B$) are excluded.

31.   If the relative position in time of two out of the three witnesses is known, it is again the case that IVa and IVc will fit any of the six chronologically ordered pairs. IVb and IIc permit four such pairs per tree (for instance $B \rightarrowtail A$, $A \rightarrowtail C$, $C \rightarrowtail A$, $B \rightarrowtail C$ both for nos. 5 and 21). IIa allows five pairs per tree (only $C \rightarrowtail B$ is excluded for no. 10). IIb allows three pairs (for no. 16, $A \rightarrowtail B$, $A \rightarrowtail C$, $B \rightarrowtail C$).

For any one Quentin intermediary, say B, those two chronologically ordered pairs in which the intermediary is the more recent partner (say, $A \rightarrowtail B$, $C \rightarrowtail B$) are compatible with one IIb tree (here nos. 16 or 17, respectively) each. Each of the other four pairs ($B \rightarrowtail A$, $A \rightarrowtail C$, $C \rightarrowtail A$, $B \rightarrowtail C$) is compatible with two IIa trees (nos. 10, 11), one IIb tree (nos. 17, 16, 17, 16, respectively), and one IIc tree (no. 21).

32.   It follows from the preceding sections that

(α) the tabulation of variants determines whether the stemma for three given witnesses is any one of the seven noded trees, or any one of the five noded trees in which that manuscript against which the other two never agree occupies the 'intermediary' position (see Sections 11–16);

(β) knowledge of the chronological order in which two out of the three witnesses came into existence narrows the choice to six noded stemmata out of seven (in IVb the manuscript functioning as archetype cannot be the more recent partner in a pair), or to either four or two out of the five non-noded stemmata with a given 'intermediary' (see Section 31);

knowledge of the chronological order in which all three witnesses came into existence narrows the choice to five noded stemmata out of seven (in IVb the manuscript functioning as archetype must be the earliest in a triplet), or to three, two, or none of the five non-noded stemmata with a given 'intermediary' (see Section 30);

(γ) partial knowledge of which variants constitute deviation ('error', innovation) makes possible the selection of the appropriate stemma, the 'full' reconstruction of the hyparchetype (if there is a separate one), and either the 'full' or the 'partial' reconstruction of the archetype (see Sections 25–29).

33.   By way of an example, suppose that three manuscripts, arbitrarily labeled A, B, C, show the variant classes $o\ q$, $o\ r$, and $p\ q$, respectively. This makes A the Quentin intermediary, and selects nos. 8, 9; 14, 15; and 20 as possible stemmata. Suppose, moreover, that B is known to have been written before A. This leaves only nos. 8 and 14 on the list. In the latter case (no. 14), B is the archetype. In the former (no. 8), the archetype has the readings on which A agrees with B against C (o), some of the readings on which A agrees with C against B (q), some of the readings on which B stands alone against the agreement of A with C (r), but none of the readings on which C stands alone against the agreement of A with B (p). If, however, some variants can be identified as 'innovations', the stemma results directly: if p, q, and r all include some 'errors', while o does not, the tree is no. 8.

34.   It remains to comment once more on the analogy between manuscript stemmatics and the construction of family trees for languages. For this purpose it is convenient to state certain of our data as they appear to the observer of a particular line of descent. To such an observer the copy and the model, as well as the copy-model relationship between the two, are known, either because such knowledge is explicitly given, or because an algorithm (Section 32) is available to reconstruct it. Suppose that the model is our node (Y), and the copy our A implicit in no. 5 (Figure 59). Examination of the two will reveal two kinds of location: one occupied by stretches where the copy agrees with the model, and another occupied by stretches where the copy deviates from the model. Each kind might be given a label such as $s > s$ (where s is the class of those passages in Y the reading of which is maintained in A, and of those passages in A the reading of which is maintained from Y)

for the first, and $t > u$ (where t is the class of those passages in Y the reading of which is deviated from in A, and u is the class of those passages in A the reading of which deviates from Y) for the second. Instead of s, u, and t, we shall use dl, g, and f, respectively; we do so in order to bring our symbols into line with our fuller knowledge – not shared, of course, by the mere observer of Y and of A – of the other factors entering into no. 5 (Section 24). Thus, the two kinds of location are written $dl > dl$, and $g > f$. The partitioning of the class of locations into two classes presupposes a criterion to decide whether any two stretches (readings) are different or not. This may be seen as a matter of alphabetic (or other) writing. In the simplest case it is taken for granted that Y and A are written in the same alphabet (syllabary, ...). The totality of passages written in this alphabet, both in Y and in A, may, then, be considered as partitioned threefold, into dl, g, and f, according as the passages are distributed between the manuscripts.

Granting that locations can be identified (the problem is similar to that of translation alluded to in Chapter I, Section 8), we think of the notation '$dl > dl$', '$g > f$' as denoting a relation and not, in this context, a process; each expression is the name of a set of ordered pairs of particular passages one of which is in Y, the other in A. Then, g (dl in Y) alone is the domain, and f (dl in A) the counterdomain. Passages seen as they change or remain unchanged between witnesses are stretches. Each ordered pair of the relation is a location.

35.   No other diagnostic properties are claimed for the classes $dl > dl$, $g > f$; dl, g, and f. Since a passage is a given stretch in a given location in a given witness (say, the words *to be* at the beginning of Hamlet's soliloquy in a particular edition), the recurrence of identically constituted stretches is beside the point. The fact that a scribe or a printer miscopies *to be* in the specified location does not generally predispose him to miscopy, still less to miscopy identically, the same words elsewhere; where such things do happen they are considered as sources of interference with the processes under study. With a concrete example this is easy to see. Just so, as we return to formal expression, it must be kept in mind that the members of g have nothing more in common with one another than that they are passages in Y such that each one is paired, by location, with a passage in A graphemically different from it (these passages forming the class f), and vice versa. The class dl, on the other hand, may be seen as comprising two subsets, dl_Y and dl_A, such that each passage in Y which belongs to dl_Y is paired, by location, with a graphemically identical member of dl_A in A, and vice versa.

36.   Clearly, linguistic change processes are similar, though some particular such processes more so than others. Innovation in language and deviation

in copying are, as we have shown or implied, amenable to analogous bits of reasoning, along with other known processes that evolve in time, such as mutations in living organisms, especially in their biochemical genetic aspects. But the closeness, in nature as well as in the history of scholarship, of manuscript work to linguistics actually obscures rather than enhances the true analogies. It is certainly not the case that texts, written and then copied, are the true analogs of discourses (the linguists' 'connected texts'), uttered and capable of being later on re-uttered, even though written texts happen to be records of discourses or of collections of discourses. True, there is a valid parallelism between the replacement of OE *cweðan, secgan, ēam*, by *say, tell, uncle*, respectively, in the Modern English language and of course in the discourses thereof, and the class $g > f$ above; and, on the other hand, between any OE word which is said to have remained in the language, subject only to sound change, e.g. *dōn* 'do', and the class $dl > dl$.[60] But since the discourses of a later stage are not essentially just replicas of particular discourses of an earlier stage, and since linguistic reconstruction does not essentially aim at the reconstruction of particular discourses, the concept of the passage lacks a linguistic conterpart.[61] In historical linguistic work, recurrence of the replacements is not only allowed, but constitutes the fundamental datum to be considered. When a manuscript archetype is reconstructed, particular deviations, whereby a given witness has changed or jeopardized the meaning of the text, are identified and eliminated. When, on the other hand, an ancestor language is reconstructed, certain recurrent innovations, whereby a given daughter language has altered the means of conveying messages are identified and eliminated. Textual critics aim at recovering particular discourses, each with its meaning, in a known language, while historical linguists aim at recovering a language in which particular discourses with their meanings can be generated. Hence the linguist considers, in principle, ALL occurrences of such stretches as *cweðan, secgan, ēam, dōn*. When he discovers that the occurrences of *cweðan* after *be-* behave like *dōn* in remaining unchanged (*[be]queath*) rather than yielding to a different item (*say*), he will of course treat the simple verb and the compound as separate items; that is, he will in effect subdivide the occurrences of *cweðan*. But he will do so according to environments still capable of recurring from discourse to discourse, and not according to particular discourses.

37.   As long as we deal with examples of lexical change – that is, with loanwords like *uncle* < French *oncle*), with effects of semantic change like *say* and *tell*, and also with so-called analogic changes like (*shoe*)-*s* for (*shoo*)-*n* – the analogy of the alphabet (Section 34) still holds to a degree; namely, on con-

dition that we can distinguish such lexical changes from sound change (chapter I, Section 10). If no sound change has occurred during the period spanned by the line of descent, innovations are simply those forms which are phonemically different from the forms which they replace, while retentions are those that are identical. If sound change has intervened, this is to be taken into account, so that *do* and *bequeath*, with their changed phonetic-phonemic appearance, are still lexical retentions. With the sound changes themselves, that is: with those phonemic innovations which may be stated in terms of phonemic rather than morphemic environments, the matter is, of course, different. If one takes the view that sound laws state replacement relations between elements of two 'alphabets' each of which is a self-sufficient system, there is no defined alphabetic continuity, and indeed no relation between any symbol in the older stage alphabet and any symbol in the later stage alphabet beyond the replacement relation itself (Chapter I, Section 7), Less stringent views have been proposed, but, whatever their merits may be, it is desirable to be able to seize upon those properties of sound change which remain defined under the most stringent interpretation.

38.   It is the merger processes which most clearly satisfy this requirement. A homonym-producing merger will appear as such under any one of several phonetic-phonemic notations chosen; in particular, its recognition is neither furthered nor hampered by any effort to choose phonemicizations of the two stages in such a way as to bring out phonetic or otherwise systematic resemblances from system to system. If both a and b go to m (Section 4), and if $m < a$ and $m < b$ occur in the same environment, there is merger, regardless, for example, of the feature combinations which a, b, and m may represent. This is one of the reasons why phonemic merger, in spite of certain weaknesses that attach to the use of phonological data for purposes of historical inference, has become the prototype of linguistic innovation. The earliest oscillation $t > d > t$ in the history of the German word for 'wind' (Chapter I, Section 20) may be a (possibly remarkable) reversion, physically speaking, to the starting point. But more important and more clearcut is the circumstance that each step is also marked by a merger, with possible loss of lexical contrast. At the second stage Germanic d is the merger product of Indo-European t (after unaccented syllable) and Indo-European dh; and at the third stage, as this d goes to Old High German t, there are environments – namely, after s or before r, or both – where Germanic t, too, appears as Old High German t. Thus, if we consider the vicissitudes of Indo-European t in an appropriately chosen context (namely, say, after an unaccented syllable and before r) we have

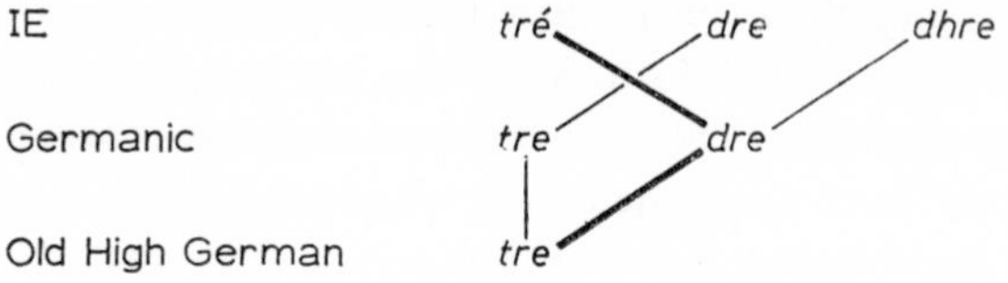

IE   tré   dre   dhre

Germanic   tre   dre

Old High German   tre

Fig. 70.

where even a different vertical alignment, that is, a different interpretation of phonetic identities from stage to stage, would leave the two nodes and their relationship intact.[62]

39.   What is more, phonological mergers can be identified internally by the comparative method in the narrower sense of the term (see Section 5). As we turn from the business of studying innovations along a known line of descent to the situation analogous to that which is characteristic of most of the three-witness problems examined earlier, this advantage is paramount, since a knowledge of what is innovated rather than retained in a collection of related languages allows us to reverse the reasoning and to retrieve the lines of descent. There may be something paradoxical in the fact that the classical, operative phonological innovation is not a new entity in the inventory – say, a newly formed distinctive feature association, an additional phoneme or cluster – but a loss of contrast, a diminution rather than an increment. Yet this is precisely what lends the phonological argument its strength. Compare with this the much lesser power of ordinary lexical or grammatical innovation, with its straightforward resemblance to what happens in manuscript history – witness the complaint that 'it is often difficult to know what is retention and what is innovation, for a semantic change in one direction can often just as easily occur in reverse fashion'.[63]

40.   There are some other imperfect parallelisms worth reflecting on. For a scribe to deviate from his model constitutes, in many cultural contexts, failure (mistake or falsification); for the speakers of a language to adopt an innovation is not an act to be valued one way or the other, unless change is seen as corruption (or progress). Still, there have been attempts at explaining linguistic change by surmising that some or most changes are the effect of imperfect adjustment in bidialectal contact.[64] A more important matter is the function of time and the discreteness of events in time. In the case of manuscripts the vertices of the stemma (whether directly known or inferred) represent the more or less clearly delimited acts of making copies. As a copy is made, all deviations are produced at once. In language the notion of one change event is, as we have seen, difficult and vague. For this reason, the

stages along a line of descent in a manuscript history are created by that very history, whereas the identification of stages in language descent depends on the accidents of preservation, on the interpretation of relative chronologies, or on the reconstruction of points in time at which a language community split up in a more or less neat fashion.[65] In certain respects linguistic change goes forward at all times, so that it has seemed reasonable to speculate that the extent of change undergone may provide a measure of the time elapsed. Similar speculation for manuscript histories has been rejected.[66] It is certainly true that if the same model gives rise to a chain of copies, each one adding its share of deviation, and then is itself copied once again,

Fig. 71.

the extent of deviation found at the end of the chain may be expected to be greater than that found in the independent copy, no matter how much more recent the latter is. In fact, while in the case of language distance along a path of descent is appropriately measured by a time scale, regardless of the number of vertices encountered, distance along a path of descent in manuscript history should, contrariwise, be measured in vertices, regardless of the length of time. This is the meaning of the maxim 'recentiores non deteriores'.[67] None of this alters the importance of the relative chronology of copying down one and the same line of descent (Section 30).[68] In this respect the analogy between languages and manuscripts remains valid. If there is information about the chronological order in which two or three out of the three languages were recorded, this will circumscribe the choice among the 22 trees in the same way in which this is true of manuscripts of known relative age (Sections 30, 31).

41.   This brings to mind a special case. Languages may be found recorded SIMULTANEOUSLY; typically so in fields where most or all of the material comes from fresh field work and not from old documents. These given languages are then simultaneous, inasmuch as they are, both or all of them, current. Now, it is clear that simultaneity is the same as absence of chronological ordering; for two simultaneous languages on one line of descent would have to be identical. If they differ, they cannot simply be linked by one such line.

Therefore, if our three given languages are contemporary, they can only fit the trees of the types IVa (nos. 1, 2, 3) and IVc (no. 7).

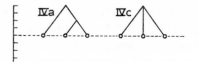

Fig. 72.

If two are contemporary, while the third is known to be, or may be, older, there are, in addition to these same trees, one IVb tree, two IIa trees, and one IIc tree for each such pair (e.g., for A and B: nos. 1, 2, 3, 6, 7, 12, 13, 22); there is no IIb tree. Note that only the non-intermediaries can be simultaneous in a IIa or IIc Quentin tree.

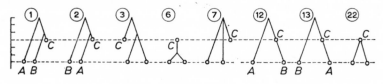

Fig. 73.

42. Trifurcation in manuscript history carries implications quite different from those in language history. Since no accident of physical simultaneity is involved, it is not implausible for one manuscript – especially a prestigious one – to be copied twice over again. That a finding of trifurcation (or of a split of even higher degree) has in fact so seldom been reported in concrete text histories is therefore striking; explanations vary.[69] Trifurcation of a language, on the other hand, to be historically real, would have to have a background of near-simultaneous dispersal of the speech community into more or less isolated offshoots. One would then have to ask under what typical conditions such dispersal is to be expected.

Language trifurcation is often posited. Examination may show, however, that the features shared by two or by all three pairs of daughter languages against each third, unpaired language are, in part, innovations. This fails to fit not only IVc (the trifurcated tree) but the other trees as well (Section 24). The tree model with all its simplifying conditions is therefore not really applicable, and the picture of dispersal can be maintained only at the cost of blaming the sharing on independent identical development, or on diffusion (borrowing) within the language family.[70] The latter suspicion is strengthened when we find only two and not all three pairs carrying innovations. Suppose that the pairs A-B and A-C do carry innovations, while

B-C does not; this might suggest that the speakers of *B* and *C* were not in contact with each other. Naturally, these interpretations are of interest to the general historian, especially when they add to knowledge available from other indications.

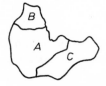

Fig. 74.

43.   This is only a special case of a much wider variety of possible cases in which independent duplication and diffusion operate. On the whole, the analogies are close. The manuscript counterpart of linguistic diffusion is seen in contamination, when scribes copy from more than one model. The extraordinary formal difficulties caused thereby are well known.[71] As for separate identical deviation, the scribal equivalent is also clear: two scribes may make the same mistake or the same intended improvement. Both in linguistics and in textual stemmatics a great deal depends on the criteria whereby given linguistic changes or scribal departures are declared significant or trivial – that is, less likely or more likely to be duplicated. These criteria have been widely discussed. For example, established styles or fashions in orthography may make identical respellings completely trivial. A rare name or word, and in fact any lectio difficilior may lead more than one copyist to the same obvious trivialization. And if it were possible to define more clearly the factors of naturalness, markedness, directionality, and the areally or universally active forces which have been said to control the incidence and direction of sound change, the chances of pinpointing significant and unlikely to be duplicated processes would indeed be bright. Change processes other than sound change, with the larger choices that exist where syntax and lexicon are involved, would seem to be less subject to the danger of independent duplication; but this has to be balanced against the greater difficulty in telling innovation from retention.

CHAPTER III

NOTES ON GLOTTOCHRONOLOGICAL TREES

1. Trees may be studied without giving any meaning to the length of the edges connecting the vertices in the customary tree diagrams. The twenty-two different three-witness trees above (Figure 59) are, in fact, twenty-two such non-metrical objects. As shown, they lend themselves to representing many of the characteristic relationships that exist among manuscripts or among languages. These are, in part, relationships in time. Along any one path of descent each edge of a rooted tree from vertex to vertex – L-point, node, root point – represents, among other things, a time difference, with the vertex nearer the root point depicting the older stage and the one farther away from it the later stage. The direction away from the root point corresponds to the downward flow of time. In this view, edges are only defined by their (are, in fact, pairs of) vertices. Their length is not open to interpretation any more than their curvature when drawn on a two-dimensional surface, or the angle at which they are drawn with regard to one another on such a surface.

2. Vertices located on different paths of descent are not ordered in a way which leads to a chronological interpretation. When a time scale, originating at the root point, was added to the array, the purpose was still not to measure the length of the edges absolutely (see note 76); it was only to illustrate possible relative positions in which time vertices in general, including those not joined by a path of descent, can occupy precisely by virtue of the fact that they are not ordered. To let vertices assume these positions it is, to be sure, necessary graphically to lengthen and shorten the edges.

3. It is, however, also possible to consider trees characterized not only by their non-metrical properties, but, in addition, by the length of their edges. A measure of justification for this lies in the suggestion that there may be a relation between a lapse of time and the EXTENT of linguistic change which it produces (Chapter II, Section 40). How to quantify the effects of change is another matter. The most elaborate effort along the lines of finding a workable parameter has been in the field of lexicostatistics, with certain aspects of vocabulary replacement within some continuing semantic framework the subject of observation.[72] The merits and difficulties of this approach are still debated. We shall here merely assume – and that for the sake of argument only – that some acceptable index of diversity due to the passage of time has been identified and can be used to reconstruct time intervals.[73]

4.   If it were statistically meaningful and true to say, for example, that on the average, a certain fraction – say, 80% – of some part of the vocabulary is retained after a certain time interval – say t years –; and if it were also true that after another t years 80% of the vocabulary thus retained would be retained in turn, the total average retention after 2 t years would be 80% of 80% or 64%:[74]

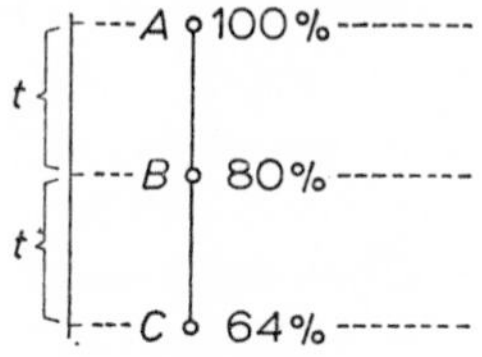

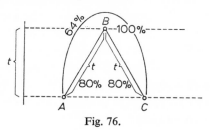

Fig. 75.

Note that the numerical relationship between the stages (e.g., A and C) is symmetrical. Of hundred semantic slots, 64% are filled by the same item in A and in C, whereas in the case of the remaining 36 meaning A and C differ, each exhibiting a particular variant. It may be the case that some of the particular items in C (and none in A) are recognizable as innovations (because they are foreign loanwords, or formed by a more productive process of word derivation, etc.), but there is nothing in the numerical data alone to indicate direction in time. The finding is simply that C and A are removed from each other by a DISTANCE of 2 t.

5.   Moreover, consider an ancestor, B, with two separate descendants, A and C. As the interval t elapses, both A and C retain 80% of the vocabulary of B. If it were true that all items in the 'basic' vocabulary are equally prone to be replaced, the vocabulary which A and C still share would once again be 80% of 80%, or 64%.[75] In short, our indices, if they accomplish what is implied, seem to yield the distance between the points (languages) without regard to the location of the root point and consequently for the direction of time. It is impossible to state whether this direction is upward or downward a line of descent, and indeed whether it is not reversed as the root point is passed in the pursuit of a collateral relationship. Essentially what matters is the non-rooted shape of the metrical tree.

Fig. 76.

6.   Let us note the metrical properties of a given noded three-witness tree, non-rooted, (Chapter II, Section 8):

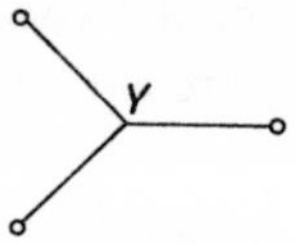

Fig. 77.

as follows:

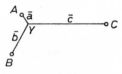

Fig. 78.

where $\bar{a}$, $\bar{b}$, and $\bar{c}$, are the lengths of the edges (measured in t's)[76] $\overline{AY}$, $\overline{BY}$, and $\overline{CY}$, respectively. Since we think of A, B, and C as representing given languages (complete with given vocabularies to analyze statistically, if that is the datum we wish to use), we may also think of their distances $\overline{AB}$, $\overline{AC}$, and $\overline{BC}$ as given. If so, it is possible to fix the metrical position of the node, Y, to the other points, since, according to construction,

$$\overline{AC}=\overline{AB}+\overline{BC}-2\overline{YB} \quad \text{[and, of course, also}$$
$$\overline{AB}=\overline{AC}+\overline{BC}-2\overline{YC}, \quad \text{and}$$
$$\overline{BC}=\overline{AB}+\overline{AC}-2\overline{YA}],$$

or

$$\bar{b}=\overline{YB}=\tfrac{1}{2}(\overline{AB}+\overline{BC}-\overline{AC}) \quad \text{[as well as}$$
$$\bar{c}=\overline{YC}=\tfrac{1}{2}(\overline{AC}+\overline{BC}-\overline{AB}), \quad \text{and}$$
$$\bar{a}=\overline{YA}=\tfrac{1}{2}(\overline{AB}+\overline{AC}-\overline{BC})].$$

For example, let the distances between A, B, and C be measured as

	B	C
A	7	10
B		13

Fig. 79.

Then,

$$\bar{b}=\tfrac{1}{2}(7+13-10)=5,$$
$$\bar{c}=\tfrac{1}{2}(10+13-7)=8,$$
$$\bar{a}=\tfrac{1}{2}(7+10-13)=2.$$

Note that in a noded tree such as the one here considered, the distances will be triangular numbers (that is, the sum of any two will exceed the third), or the expressions within the parentheses will fail to be positive. This is of course guaranteed by the circumstance that $\overline{AB}+\overline{BC}$, being, in fact, $(\bar{a}+\bar{b})+(\bar{b}+\bar{c})$, is greater by $2\bar{b}$ than $\bar{a}+\bar{c}$ or $\overline{AC}$, etc.

In a non-noded tree the distance from Y to the intermediary, say C, is zero, so that $\overline{AC}+\overline{BC}=\overline{AB}$.

7.   Now let there be an edge linking A and B, the distance being $\bar{d}$:

Fig. 80.

Let it further be given that the records from which A is known are $\frac{1}{4}\bar{d}$ older than the records of B. This allows us to place the ancestor, X, as follows:

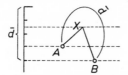

Fig. 81.

that is, X is $\frac{1}{2}(\bar{d}-\frac{1}{4}\bar{d})=\frac{3}{8}\bar{d}$ older than A. More generally, as the time difference between two languages ranges from zero (with both languages contemporary) to $\bar{d}$ (with one the older stage of the other), if the given time difference is $\bar{d}/\delta$, X lies at the depth $\frac{1}{2}(\bar{d}-\bar{d}/\delta)$ from the older language, and at the depth of $\frac{1}{2}(\bar{d}+\bar{d}/\delta)$ from the later language.

Information concerning the position in time of two languages exists, in particular, when two languages are directly observable in the field, and hence simultaneous (Chapter II, Section 41). In this case, the kind of problem of which an example has just been given assumes a simpler form. If A and B are simultaneous, and differ by $\bar{d}$, the ancestor has a time depth of $\frac{1}{2}\bar{d}$.

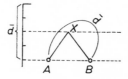

Fig. 82.

8. Generally (that is, in the noded tree) the distances for A, B, and C are

	B	C
A	$\bar{a}+\bar{b}$	$\bar{a}+\bar{c}$
B		$\bar{b}+\bar{c}$

Fig. 83.

(Section 6). If A, B, and C, are simultaneous, they enter either into the IVc tree (no. 7) or into one of the IVa trees (nos. 1, 2, 3). In the case of the IVc tree, where the ancestor coincides with the node, $\bar{a}$, $\bar{b}$, and $\bar{c}$ are equal to one another, so that

	B	C
A	$2\bar{a}$	$2\bar{a}$
B		$2\bar{a}$

Fig. 84.

If the tree is a IVa one (e.g., no. 3), $\bar{a}$ equals $\bar{b}$, and the distances are

	B	C
A	$2\bar{a}$	$\bar{a}+\bar{c}$
B		$\bar{a}+\bar{c}$

Fig. 85.

9. There are eight trees which will accommodate two simultaneous languages out of three languages (the third to be thought of as earlier than the other two). The eight trees for simultaneous A, B are listed above (Figure 73). Of these, nos. 12, 13, and 22, are non-noded. Since in these trees the node Y has disappeared as a separate entity by coinciding with the intermediary (here C), $\bar{c}$ equals zero, and the distances, as appears clearly from the tree diagram, are

	B	C
A	$\bar{a}+\bar{b}$	$\bar{a}$
B		$\bar{b}$

Fig. 86.

This describes nos. 12 or 13, according as $\bar{a}$ is greater or less than $\bar{b}$. In either case the ancestral depth from A, B is $\frac{1}{2}(\bar{a}+\bar{b})$. If $\bar{a}=\bar{b}$, the tree is no. 22,

	B	C
A	$2\bar{a}$	$\bar{a}$
B		$\bar{a}$

Fig. 87.

The time depth for the ancestor, X, is $\frac{1}{2}(\bar{a}+\bar{a})=\bar{a}$ from A, B.

Of the noded trees let us first consider nos. 1 and 2 (IVa, with the independently related language and one of the subancestrally related languages being
simultaneous, so that the two simultaneous languages are not dominated
by the node). Note that $\bar{c}$ is less than $\bar{a}$ and less than $\bar{b}$; in no. 1, $\bar{a}$ is greater
than $\bar{b}$; in no. 2, $\bar{b}$ is greater than $\bar{a}$. The depth of X (from A, B) is $\frac{1}{2}(\bar{a}+\bar{b})$.
The remaining trees – nos. 3 (IVa, with the two subancestrally related lan-
guages being simultaneous), 6 (IVb) and 7 (IVc) – are likewise noded, with the
two simultaneous languages issuing from the node itself.[77] Consequently,
$\bar{a}=\bar{b}$. In no. 3, $\bar{c}$ is greater than $\bar{a}$; in no. 7, $\bar{c}$ is less than $\bar{a}$ (so long as C
antedates A, B). The table of the distances is

	B	C
A	$2\bar{a}$	$\bar{a}+\bar{c}$
B		$\bar{a}+\bar{c}$

Fig. 88.

precisely as in the formula for three simultaneous languages in IVa above
(Figure 85). The time depth, from A, B, for X is $\bar{a}+\bar{c}$ for no. 6, and $\bar{a}$ for no.
7. In the case of no. 3, X occupies a position in the stretch in between: it has
a depth greater than $\bar{a}$ and less than $\bar{a}+\bar{c}$ from A, B.

10.   In sum, when two simultaneous languages A and B (for example, two
languages recorded in the field) need to be fitted into a tree with a third,
possibly earlier, language C (perhaps one known from records of uncertain
antiquity, or reconstructed from witnesses within the family), the following
combinations of data may be encountered.

(α) The three distances $\overline{AB}$, $\overline{AC}$, and $\overline{BC}$, are triangular (Section 6) and, in
particular, equal to one another. Each distance is found[78] to measure $2\bar{a}$. Then
C is either contemporary as well (Section 8), the tree being no. 7; or C
has a time depth of $2\bar{a}$ with regard to A and B, and the tree is no. 6, with C as
the ancestor; or C has a time depth less than $2\bar{a}$ with regard to A, B, and
the tree is no. 3.

(β) The three distances are triangular. $\overline{AB}$ is equal to one of the other
two and greater than the third. The first two distances are found to measure
$\bar{a}+\bar{b}$, the third distance, $2\bar{b}$ or $2\bar{a}$. C is contemporary as well. The tree is either
no. 1 or no. 2, according as it is $\overline{AC}$ or $\overline{BC}$ that equals $\overline{AB}$.

(γ) The three distances are triangular. $\overline{AB}$ is not equal to the other two
distances, which are, however, equal to each other. $\overline{AB}$ is found to measure
$2\bar{a}$; the other two distances are found to measure $\bar{a}+\bar{c}$. If $\overline{AB}$ is less than each
of the other two, the tree is either no. 3, in which case C has a time depth less
than $\bar{a}+\bar{c}$ from, and may be contemporary with, A and B; or it is no. 6, with

C as the ancestor. If $\overline{AB}$ is greater than each of the other two distances, the tree is either no. 7, with the time depth of C being $\bar{a}-\bar{c}$; or no. 3, with the time depth of $\bar{c}$ greater than $\bar{a}-\bar{c}$ and less than $\bar{a}+\bar{c}$ from A and B; or it is once again no. 6, with C as the ancestor.

(δ) The three distances are triangular, with no two equaling each other. They are found to be $\bar{a}+\bar{b}$, $\bar{a}+\bar{c}$, and $\bar{b}+\bar{c}$, respectively (Section 6). The tree is no. 1, if $\bar{a}$ is greater than $\bar{b}$, and no. 2, if $\bar{b}$ is greater than $\bar{a}$, with C at depth $\bar{c}-\bar{b}$ and $\bar{c}-\bar{a}$, respectively, from A and B.

(ε) The three distances miss being triangular by satisfying the limiting condition only (Section 6): $\overline{AB}=\bar{a}+\bar{b}$, but $\overline{AC}=\bar{a}$, and $\overline{BC}=\bar{b}$. In other words, $\bar{c}$ equals zero, and the tree is non-noded, with C in the intermediary position. If $\bar{a}$ is greater than $\bar{b}$, the time depth of C with respect to A and B is $\bar{b}$, and the tree is no. 12; if $\bar{b}$ is greater than $\bar{a}$, the time depth of C is $\bar{a}$, and the tree is no. 13.

(ζ) The three distances miss being triangular by meeting the limiting condition only; again, $\overline{AB}=\overline{AC}+\overline{BC}$. In addition, $\overline{AC}=\overline{BC}$, so that the values are $2\bar{a}$, $\bar{a}$, and $\bar{a}$, respectively. The (non-noded) tree is no. 22; the time depth of C (which is the ancestor), from A, B, is $\bar{a}$.

To sum up:

If A and B are contemporary, and C is either contemporary as well, or earlier, and if*

$$\overline{AC}>\overline{BC},$$
$$\overline{AB}\geq\overline{AC}, \text{ and}$$
$\overline{AB}>\overline{BC}$, the tree is no. 1 ($\beta$, δ); but if, in particular,
$\overline{AC}+\overline{BC}=\overline{AB}$, the tree is no. 12 ($\varepsilon$);

if $\overline{AC}<\overline{BC},$
$\overline{AB}>\overline{AC}, \text{ and}$
$\overline{AB}\geq\overline{BC}$, the tree is no. 2 ($\beta$, δ); but if, in particular,
$\overline{AC}+\overline{BC}=\overline{AB}$, the tree is no. 13 ($\varepsilon$);

if $\overline{AC}=\overline{BC}, \text{ and}$
$\overline{AB}\geq\overline{AC}$, $\overline{BC}$, the tree is no. 3 or no. 6 or no. 7 (α, γ); but if, in particular, $\overline{AC}+\overline{BC}=\overline{AB}$, the tree is no. 22 ($\zeta$);

if $\overline{AC}=\overline{BC}, \text{ and}$
$\overline{AB}<\overline{AC}$, $\overline{BC}$, the tree is no. 3 or no. 6 (γ).

11.   The characteristics listed in Section 10 only fit triads of languages such that at least two languages ('A', 'B') are simultaneous.

Note that a non-noded tree with the characteristics $2\bar{a}$, $\bar{a}$, and $\bar{a}$ may indeed

* Note that $>$, $<$ in this section stand for 'greater, less than'.

be no. 22 with simultaneous non-intermediaries (Section 10 ζ). It may, however, also be either no. 12 or 13 with the ancestor at the depth $\bar{x}$ with respect
to C, and with A earlier than B (no. 12), or B earlier than A (no. 13), by the
amount $2\bar{x}$ (Figure 89); or it may be no. 18 or 19 (IIb trees incapable of
accommodating simultaneities) [79] with A or B, respectively, as the ancestor,
and C at the chronological half-way mark.

12. In conclusion it may be useful to compare the three-witness trees built
on an assumed – and for all that is known too optimistically assumed – knowledge of glottochronological distances, with the classical trees attained
through the comparative method. These trees are non-metrical; all that
counts is the relation between the root point, the nodes, and the remaining
points as they are linked by edges. Unlike the glottochronological trees,
classical comparative trees have directed edges, since innovations can be

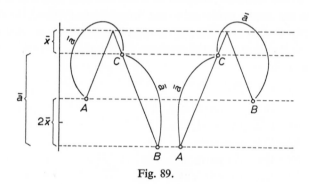

Fig. 89.

distinguished from retentions in the very process of setting up the correspondences.[80] As we review the matrices that lead to the reconstruction or recognition of the six tree types of Figure 59, we find a certain interesting parallelism with the procedures developed above for glottochronological trees.

13. If three languages A, B, and C are subjected to the comparative method
by pairs, the following two cases may arise: (a) the three pairs yield one and
the same reconstruction, or (b) two pairs yield identical reconstructions,
while the third is different. In the first case, the ancestor may (a1) differ, or
not differ (a2) from one of the given languages. In the second case, there are
four possibilities: both the two-pair ancestor and the one-pair ancestor
differ from any of the three given languages (b1); the two-pair ancestor is
identical with one of the given languages, while the one-pair ancestor is not
(b2); the one-pair ancestor is identical with one of the given languages, while
the two-pair ancestor is not (b3); both ancestors are identical with one given

language each (*b4*). If the three-pair or two-pair ancestor is labeled *X*, and
the one-pair ancestor, *Y*, we may summarize:[81]

a1

	B	C
A	X	X
B		X

a2

	B	C
A	A	A
B		A

b1

	B	C
A	X	X
B		Y

b2

	B	C
A	A	A
B		Y

b3

	B	C
A	X	X
B		B

b4

	B	C
A	A	A
B		B

Fig. 90.

Moreover, if the two-pair ancestor and the one-pair ancestor found in the
same matrix are in turn subjected to the comparative method, the reconstruction is identical with the two-pair ancestor not only in *a2* and *b4*, but in
general. It is clear that when the trees are drawn, they correspond to those in
Figure 59 as follows:

$a1 = $ IVc   (7)
$a2 = $ IIc   (in particular, 20)
$b1 = $ IVa   (in particular, 1)
$b2 = $ IVb   (in particular, 4)
$b3 = $ IIa   (in particular, 10)
$b4 = $ IIb   (in particular, 16).

Here, as in the case of the glottochronological trees for simultaneous languages (Section 10) the pattern according to which language pairs share or
fail to share relationships is interpreted chronologically. In glottochronology,
it is the 'distance' between the members of the pair which is considered. In
the field of classical comparative reconstruction it is the direction of the
linkage expressed in the form of a reconstruction, that is, of the collection of
retentions in the two languages.

BIBLIOGRAPHY

Andersen, H., 1969, 'A Study in Diachronic Morphophonemics: The Ukrainian Prefixes', *Language* **45**, 807–31.

Andersen, H., 1948, 'Diphthongization', *Language* **48**, 11–50.

Anttila, R., 1972, *An Introduction to Historical and Comparative Linguistics*, Macmillan, New York.

Arlotto, A., 1972, *Introduction to Historical Linguistics*, Houghton Mifflin Company, Boston.

Austin, W. M., 1957, 'Criteria for Phonetic Similarity', *Language* **33**, 538–43.

Bennett, W. H., 1968, 'The Operation and Relative Chronology of Verner's Law', *Language* **44**, 219–23.

Bonfante, G., 1947, 'The Neolinguistic Position', *Language* **23**, 344–75.

Bräuer, H., 1961, *Slavische Sprachwissenschaft*, Vol. 1, Walter De Gruyter & Co., Berlin.

Bright, W. (ed.), 1966, *Sociolinguistics*, Mouton & Co., The Hague, Paris.

Buck, C. D., 1955, *The Greek Dialects*, University of Chicago Press, Chicago.

Chafe, W. L., 1968, 'The Ordering of Phonological Rules', *IJAL* **34**, 115–36.

Chomsky, N. and Halle, M., 1968, 'The Sound Pattern of English', Harper & Row, New York.

Dobson, A. J., 1969, 'Lexicostatistical Grouping', *Anthropological Linguistics* **11**, 216–21.

Dyen, I., 1969, 'Reconstruction, the Comparative Method, and the Proto-Language Uniformity Assumption', *Language* **45**, 499–518.

Dyen, I., 1972, 'Non-gradual Regular Phonetic Changes Involving Sibilants', in J. M. C. Thomas and L. Bernot (eds.), *Langue et techniques: nature et societé*, I., Klincksieck, Paris, pp. 95–99.

Dyen, I., James, A. T., and Cole, J. W. L., 1967, 'Language Divergence and Estimated Word Retention Rate', *Language* **43**, 150–71.

Gavare, R., 1972, *Graph Description of Linguistic Structures*, Almqvist & Wiksell, Stockholm.

Götze, A., 1923, 'Relative Chronologie von Lauterscheinungen im Italischen', *Indogermanische Forschungen* **41**, 78–149.

Greenberg, J., 1957, *Essays in Linguistics*, University of Chicago Press, Chicago.

Greenberg, J. (ed.), 1963; 1966, *Universals of Language*, M.I.T. Press, Cambridge, Mass.

Greg, W. W., 1927, *The Calculus of Variants*, Oxford University Press, Oxford.

Hill, A. A., 1950–1, 'Some Postulates for Distributional Study of Texts', *Studies in Bibliography* (Papers of the Bibliographical Society of the University of Virginia) **3**, 63–95.

Hill, A. A., 1970, 'Trees of Descent in Linguistics and Textual Criticism', *Studia Anglica Posnaniensia* **3**, 3–12.

Hoenigswald, H. M., 1943–4, 'Internal Reconstruction', *Studies in Linguistics* **2**, 78–87.

Hoenigswald, H. M., 1952, 'The Phonology of Dialect Borrowing', *Studies in Linguistics* **10**, 1–5.

Hoenigswald, H. M., 1959, 'Some Uses of Nothing', *Language* **35**, 409–420.

Hoenigswald, H. M., 1960, *Language Change and Linguistic Reconstruction*, University of Chicago Press, Chicago.

Hoenigswald, 1966, 'Criteria for the Subgrouping of Languages', in H. Birnbaum and J. Puhvel (eds.), *Ancient Indo-European Dialects*, University of California Press, Berkeley and Los Angeles, pp. 1–12.

Hoenigswald, H. M., 1973, 'The Comparative Method', in T. A. Sebeok, H. M. Hoenigswald, and R. E. Longacre (eds.), *Current Trends in Linguistics*, Vol. 11, Mouton, The Hague.

Jespersen, O., 1897–9, *Fonetik*, Copenhagen, Schubothe.

King, R. D., 1969, *Historical Linguistics and Generative Grammar*, Prentice-Hall, Englewood Cliffs.

King, R. D., 1971, 'Historical Linguistics', in W. O. Dingwall (ed.), *A Survey of Linguistic Science*, University of Maryland, College Park, Md., pp. 576–649.

Kiparsky, P., 1968, 'Linguistic Universals and Linguistic Change', in E. Bach and R. T, Harms (eds.), *Universals in Linguistic Theory*, Holt, Rinehart and Winston, New York. pp. 170–202.

Klinghardt, H., 1887, *Artikulations- und Hörübungen*, Cöthen, Schulze.

Kuryłowicz, J., 1973, 'Internal Reconstruction', in T. A. Sebeok, H. M. Hoenigswald, and R. E. Longacre (eds.), *Current Trends in Linguistics*, Vol. 11, Mouton, The Hague.

Labov, W., 1971, 'Methodology', in W. O. Dingwall (ed.), *A Survey of Linguistic Science*, University of Maryland, College Park Md., pp. 412–497.

Labov, W., 1972, 'The Internal Evolution of Linguistic Rules', in R. P. Stockwell and R. K. S. Macaulay (eds.), *Linguistic Change and Generative Theory*, Indiana University Press, Bloomington, pp. 101–71.

Labov, W., 1973, 'The Social Setting of Linguistic Change', in T. A. Sebeok, H. M. Hoenigswald, and R. E. Longacre (eds.), *Current Trends in Linguistics*, Vol. 11, Mouton, The Hague.

Lehmann, W. P., 1972, *Descriptive Linguistics*, Random House, New York.

Leumann, M., 1963, *Kleine Schriften*, Artemis, Zürich, Stuttgart.

Lieb, H.-H., 1968, *Communication Complexes and Their Stages*, Mouton, The Hague.

Lyons, J., 1968, *Introduction to Theoretical Linguistics*, Cambridge University Press, Cambridge.

Maas, P., 1960, *Textkritik*, 4th edition, Teubner, Leipzig.

Marckwardt, A. L., 1967, 'Lexical Distribution in Modern English *say* and *tell*', in W. M. Austin (ed.), *Papers in Linguistics in Honor of Léon Dostert*, Mouton, The Hague, pp. 118–22.

Martinet, A., 1955, *Économie des changements phonétiques*, Francke, Berne.

Meillet, A., 1933, 'Review of Bloomfield, L., Language', *Bulletin de la Société de Linguistique* **34**, 1–2. Reprinted in C. F. Hockett (ed.), *A Leonard Bloomfield Anthology*, Indiana University Press, Bloomington, pp. 264–5.

Meyer-Lübke, W., 1920, *Einführung in das Studium der Romanischen Sprachwissenschaft*, Winter, Heidelberg.

Naert, P., 1941, 'Des mutations *ct*, *cs*>*pt*, *ps*; *gn*>*mn* et *mn*>*un* en roumain', *Archiv für Lexikographie* **2**, 247–57.

Ore, O., 1962, *Theory of Graphs*, American Mathematical Society, Providence.

Pasquali, G., 1962, *Storia della tradizione e critica del testo*, LeMonnier, Florence.

Porzig, W., 1954, *Die Gliederung des Indogermanischen Sprachgebiets*, Winter, Heidelberg.

Postal, P. M., 1968, *Aspects of Phonological Theory*, Harper & Row, New York.

Prokosch, E., 1938, *A Comparative Germanic Grammar*, Linguistic Society of America, Baltimore.

Quentin, Dom H., 1926, *Essais de critique textuelle (ecdotique)*, Paris.

Reichstein, R., 1960, 'Études des variations sociales et géographiques des faits linguistiques', *Word* **16**, 55–95.

Sankoff, D., 1973, 'Mathematical Developments in Lexicostatistical Theory', in T. A. Sebeok, H. M. Hoenigswald, and R. E. Longacre (eds.), *Current Trends in Linguistics*, Vol. 11, Mouton, The Hague.

Shapiro, M., 1972, 'Explorations into markedness', *Language* **48**, 343–64.

Sjöstedt, G., 1936, *Studier över r-ljuden i sydskandinaviska mål*, Ohlsson, Lund.

Streitberg, W., 1896, *Urgermanische Grammatik*, Winter, Heidelberg.

Venneman, T., 1972, 'Sound Change and Markedness Theory: On the History of the German Consonant System', in R. P. Stockwell and R. K. S. Macaulay (eds.), *Linguistic Change and Generative Theory*, Indiana University Press, Bloomington, pp. 230–74.

Wang, W. S.-Y., 1969, 'Competing Changes as a Cause of Residue', *Language* **45**, 9–25.

NOTES TO CHAPTERS I–III

¹ It should be understood throughout that examples are sometimes given in simplified form. Note the abbreviations I(ndo-)E(uropean), E(nglish), O(ld) E(nglish), NE = Modern English. Also, > = becomes, < = comes from, # = pause, * = reconstructed.

² On ⊗ see Sections 6, 7.

³ A discourse is a self-contained text with no formal constraints exercised upon any part of it by any part of another utterance, whether preceding or following in time. How discourses are generated is not considered here. The above statement is certainly not meant as a plea for the closed corpus and against such an argument as that made by Lyons (1968, 144ff.) When we speak of extant and recorded discourses, we have in mind critically treated (normalized, phonemicized) texts, which may have been taken from speakers, transcribed from past records that are written in some conventional script, or reconstructed. The fact that the orthographic practices of conventional scripts may, in turn, carry information about periods older than that in which the records originated ('historical spellings') is something else again.

⁴ Conventional spellings are given in italics, between ', '.

⁵ Chomsky and Halle (1968), 405–35. The term is used in many senses; see Venneman (1972) and Shapiro (1972).

⁶ About the difficulties that attach to the so-called minimal pair test as a behavioral test see Labov (1971, 430ff.) As to the merits and demerits of an autonomous, biunique phonemicization, the question cannot be whether or not a level of that kind exists in nature, but what the advantages and disadvantages of the notation are.

⁷ If we think of these as one-word discourses, with an appropriate intonation.

⁸ ⊗ always occurs in the contexts (...⊗)⊗——⊗(⊗...).

⁹ Hoenigswald (1959).

¹⁰ To be referred to briefly as the Saussurian principle.

¹¹ In its crudest form this is the so-called substratum effect. Where the two languages in contact are dialects closely resembling each other (as of course is overwhelmingly often the case), one does not usually speak of substratum. Yet the mechanics may, in part, be the same, and where they are not the same, namely in respect to the incomparably greater ease, born of mutual intelligibility and of the absence of structural obstacles, with which borrowings can be adapted, the difference in degree would seem to go quite far toward explaining the characteristic broad scope of sound change. Labov (1973) has shown how awkward it is to attribute the source function to 'prestige', because this term suggests an easy correlation or even identity with independently recognizable social or economic status. It is quite good enough to take the familiar circular view: prestigious, in language, is what is imitated. Incidentally, it would be a mistake to see more than a model in the framework used occasionally to 'reduce' sound change (and other change) to dialect borrowing (Hoenigswald, 1952). There should be no suggestion that each speaker actually speaks an immutable idiolect until he is exposed to other equally immutable idiolects. Contact is something that takes place in far subtler and more complex ways, as we learn more clearly every day. On the other hand, an increased understanding of variability does not diminish one's conviction that the classical distinction among the various change processes is not arbitrarily taxonomic but forms a system, as some phenomena seemingly different in kind from others assume their place as special cases of the latter.

¹² Comparative in a technical sense: see Chapter II, Sections 4, 39, where it is also pointed out that the prominence of argument from the phonological data, in particular, is neither accident nor blemish.

[13] Identical with regard to the presence, but not necessarily to the physical characteristics, of the contrast under discussion. — Note that the operation alluded to would be applicable both to the indigenous material of English (match NE words with OE words of like meaning and obtain, in principle, OE words; compare NE words with Modern German words and obtain 'West Germanic' – a reconstructed entity) and to the borrowed vocabulary of English (match NE words of Old French origin with Old French words and obtain Old French words; match the same English words with Italian words, and obtain Proto-Romance or Vulgar Latin; etc.).

[14] At this point the Old French material in English would be excluded from further study (except insofar as loanwords, once borrowed into the principal channel, participate in further sound change).

[15] For example, when it is found that Classical Latin shows innovations not shared by Proto-Romance. Word-final s was reintroduced into Classical Latin (not, to be sure, a regular sound change, but still definitely an innovation), but not into the Romance languages; see Meyer-Lübke (1920, 130f.).

[16] The framework is similar to that chosen, also by way of example, by Lehmann (1972, 91ff. [with references]).

[17] Hoenigswald (1943–4); Kuryłowicz (1973–4).

[18] The connection between this task and that of finding synchronic rules and their ordering is both close and delicate; King (1969). See some of the problems raised by Andersen (1969). One point should be cleared up immediately, both to put it out of the way and because it illustrates, in simple fashion, the relation between synchronic ordering and chronology. Ordinarily, split processes depend on mergers. Only and precisely as E *mother* and *brother* begin to rhyme (*mother* had d, *brother* θ in OE) has d split into δ (before unstressed *-er#*) and d (elsewhere). Only as final syllables vanish does older English θ split into θ and δ (*wreath*: *wreathe*). The merger is systematically prior but not earlier in time.

[19] A realistic case to put. In Latin, intervocalic $s > r$; in West Germanic, and also in Scandinavian, s after an unaccented syllable ends up as r. See Section 24. In Gothic the unchanged, residual allophone of s comes to stand in contrast with z through loss of the conditioning accent.

[20] Bonfante (1947, 348f.).

[21] The last two steps did not lead to stages where t and d contrast in the relevant surroundings. This is perhaps important. See Andersen (1972, 44f.) [the data are not Bühnensprache]. – There are perhaps dialects of Yiddish where *-d* at syllable end reappears, if it continues at the underlying morphophonemic level; Kiparsky (1968, 177); King (1969, 47ff.). – On [d], [ð] see note 34.

[22] But see the analysis in Labov (1972, especially 118ff., 159). The neogrammarians, while of course presenting the regularity of sound change as a finding, handled it, in fact (that is, in their substantive historical work), as a definition. Change in the principal channel of transmission (Section 12) is found to be, in part, such that it may be formulated in terms of sounds alone ('is regular'); this is labeled 'sound' change. Sound change was indeed thought of as 'regular by definition' (Labov, 1972, 108, 118). Whether this was good or not, the neogrammarians certainly meant to classify changes which require the listing of morphs or the taking into account of morph boundaries as semantic and analogical changes and not as sound changes. The problem was not so much 'sporadic' sound change (a contradiction in terms, in view of their meaning; see above) as competing regularities (does $VrsV$ become $\bar{V}rV$ or remain $VRSV$ in Greek? Are the instances of either kind tied to the existence of morph boundaries so that they can be classified as analogic change? Are there factual grounds for declaring one or the other a dialect borrowing? Etc.) Another way of commenting on the dilemma is to ask what weight is supposed to be attached to the decision, favored by some definitely post-neogrammarian authors, to call certain grammatically conditioned changes 'sound' changes. This must mean more than that all changes are alterations of sound (Postal, 1968, 231–85). To begin to use the term 'analogy' somehow in keeping with its non-technical, everyday meaning does not help to understand the past.

[23] As in the Belorussian material quoted from Ziłyński by Andersen (1972, 16f.).

[24] E. Haugen in (ed.) Bright (1966, 43).

[25] See, for instance, Reichstein (1960); also, Labov's comments, (1972, 118) on the replacement of [l'] by [j] in Gauchat's Charmey material: 'If this were the classical model of regular change, we would expect some intermediate phonetic value from generation II. But the middle generation does not show some intermediate degree of palatalization; instead Gauchat observed fluctuation between [l'] and [j].'

[26] Jespersen (1897–9, 417).

[27] Meillet (1933); Anttila (1972, 77). Arlotto (1972, 222ff.), in wishing to account for the Rumanian pt, ps from Latin ct, x, takes comfort from the possibility that both k and p (with the 'acute' apical-palatal area in between) can be specified as 'grave', so that the change is merely one from 'diffuse' (and 'grave') to 'compact' (and 'grave'). For an older interpretation, see Naert (1944). Andersen's belief (1972, 18), that 'evolutive' phonetic change must be articulatorily gradual (that is, not, or not only, gradual in regard to the number of speakers participating in it, or in the number of lexical items 'irregularly' affected), is not founded; see Wang (1969, 14). Sjöstedt (1936, 182), whom he quotes anent r in Swedish, cites Klinghardt (1897, 185ff.). But Klinghardt speaks of 'unrolled r's', while the argument applies of course to apical and uvular trills. The 'imagination' which A.'s colleagues rightly complain is strained as they are asked to think of certain change processes as gradual is not a private faculty, but presumably a rational ability to extrapolate from phonetically and typologically informed knowledge. See also Dyen (1972).

[28] Austin (1957).

[29] In spite of the skepticism that is here implied it must never be forgotten how powerful directionality can look; IE d > Germanic t > Old High German t^s; Greek $\bar{a}$ > $\bar{e}$ > i; IE s > > Germanic z > Old Scandinavian 'R' > r (an example congenial with our hypothetical model); and many more examples.

[30] In a Saussurian framework (Section 7) mergers are the cardinal events. See Chapter II, Section 38.

[31] Kiparsky (1968), Chafe (1968). The process is 'additive'.

[32] A 'drag-chain' effect to Martinet (1955, 59ff.).

[33] By implication. The matter was not specified. But note that some of the examples in footnote 29 are of the conditioned variety; that is, they involve a split. Of course, what is a conditioned sound change under one notation may be a non-conditioned one under another.

[34] Leumann (1963, 81–4), with literature, especially Götze (1923). The much belabored relationship between Grimm's and Verner's laws is similar. In the first interval, t > θ, s > s. In the second, the fricative component in θ and s is voiced after an unaccented syllable so as to produce 'd' (merging with IE 'dh'), z. The accent distinction is dropped. This is Verner's law. There is a slight, though not unsystematic, phonetic asymmetry in the fact that nd, whether from $\breve{V}nt$ ($\breve{V}$=unaccented vowel) or from ndh did apparently not have a fricative ∂ in Germanic, while $n\theta$ (from $\breve{V}nt$) did have a fricative θ, even after n. – But see Bennett (1968); θ, after all, contrasted with t.

[35] Hoenigswald (1960, 115f.) '1', '2' are shortcut notations for '1 > 101', '2 > 102', and so on, in some similar way, for the second grid in Figure 20. See Section 1.

[36] The pattern is more telling when it is embedded in a fuller table (showing other replacements from I to III) and has to be sought out.

[37] See note 32.

[38] Streitberg (1896, 103–37); Prokosch (1938, 52–78). The argument that Germanic (and Armenian) share the change dh > d with other sister groups (Iranian, Slavic, Baltic; Celtic) and that this step is, therefore, pre-Germanic (Section 16) is atomistic and letter-bound. In these four language groups dh and d merge; in Germanic (and Armenian) they do not.

[39] The second change in each arrangement is actually unconditional in that the other allophone has by then been removed. (See Section 36). Possible additional allophones, extraneous to the problem under scrutiny, are not considered here.

[40] See Hoenigswald (1960, 114) for another example, with discussion.

[41] Kiparsky (1971, 599ff.). On the devoicing rule see above, Section 20.

60   STUDIES IN FORMAL HISTORICAL LINGUISTICS

Buck (1955, 46–52). Diphthongs are not considered.
43 C. F. Hockett in (ed.) Greenberg (1963–6, 52).
44 1954, 78; see Hoenigswald (1966, 12). The alleged importance of the isogloss lies in the fact that it seems to extend over a contiguous area embracing Germanic, Albanian, Thracian, and also to cut through some more or less well established sub-families (Celtic, Baltic). By the criteria employed, some of which are being examined here, the phenomenon appears to have different antiquity in different places. This has either troubled investigators or challenged their ingenuity. As the present discussion shows, however, this may be a case of trying to know more than the data can yield. – The Slavic examples (the validity of which is not questioned) are of the following kind: Old Church Slavic *ostrъ* 'sharp', cp. Latin *ācer* 'sharp', *(medi-)ocris*, lit. 'at half height', from *k'r*; Old Church Slavic *(o-)strovъ* 'island', Polish *strumień* 'brook', cp. Greek *rhé(w)ō* (from *sr*-), Sanskrit *srávati* 'flow', from *sr*; Old Church Slavic *strada* 'toil', cp. Latin *strēnuus* 'sturdy', from *str*.
45 In classical phonemics, is the automatic *k* (if such it is) in *E sphincter, linked, sphinx*, the same, or not the same, as the /*k*/ in *link, linking*? Is it 'more similar' to these or, as a transitional glide, to Ɋ? See also Dyen (1969, 501).
46 Old Church Slavic *sramъ* 'shame', ultimately from IE **k'órmos*, cp. *E harm*, with *k'* > Slavic *s*. See Bräuer (1961, Vol. 1, 202). There is an interesting play between *t* introduced analogically into later, and Ɋ into earlier, material, which may be interpreted as a rule order change in Kiparsky's sense (1968).
47 Ore (1962, *passim*); Gavare (1972, *passim*).
48 That is, without 'contamination'.
49 Hill (1950–1).
50 Maas (1960, 10).
51 Hoenigswald (1966).
52 Always including contrast with Ɋ; see Chapter I, Section 6.
53 Maas (1960, 27). Note that, e.g.,

        and

are not different, except necessarily (but irrelevantly) on the twodimensional page. Imagine the tree as made up instead with freely pivoting wires, like a mobile, for edges. – No interpretation of any kind is at this point given to the lengths of edges as they unavoidably appear in our diagrams. But see Chapter III. On the insertion of *X* into the non-rooted tree, see Dobson (1969).
54 Hill (1950–1, 66); Quentin (1926, 66).
55 The classes are defined ONLY through one another. A reading belongs in class *d* ONLY inasmuch as *A* shares it with *B* to the exclusion of *C*; and a reading belongs in class *e* ONLY because *A* and *B* share a reading different from it. See Section 34.
56 For the reasons which are implicit in note 57. See also Sections 25, 43.
57 See Section 21. No entry in Figure 62 is meant to cover PARTICULAR pairs of variants such that neither variant is 'acceptable' (Section 25). This could come to pass only where an 'error' already in the archetype has been compounded by one copyist – a contingency which is here in general disregarded, rightly or wrongly, as being statistically recognizable. (The same holds for corruption of one an the same passage in two or more independent copies.) However, an offensive *k k k* reading (Section 12) does argue an 'error' in the archetype. Archetypes are not necessarily (authors') originals.
58 On simultaneity, see Chapter III, Section 7.
59 Read: *B* is older than *A*; *A* is older than *C*.
60 Marckwardt (1967).
61 See note 3.
62 The heavy lines in Figure 69 indicate the main development in question, with the sources

of the mergers feeding into it given by the light lines. – The 'nodes' represent mergers. They have nothing to do with the nodes of stemmata and trees.

[63] Greenberg (1957, 53).

[64] See note 11.

[65] Lieb (1968, 114ff.).

[66] Greg (1927, 9).

[67] Pasquali (1962, 43ff.); Maas (1960, 31f.).

[68] Maas (1960, 6).

[69] Maas (1960, 29f.) on J. Bédier's charge that editors shrink from recognizing trifurcation because it limits their freedom of choice between two variants.

[70] On the inadequacy of the model to depict certain types of language history, see the ample literature on the 'wave theory'. A sampling is referred to by Anttila (1972, 304ff.).

[71] Maas (1960, 8). On the importance of lacunae, see Maas (1960, 26).

[72] Sankoff (1973, *passim*), with both bibliography and discussion. I have not seen either Haigh, 'The Recovery of the Root of the Tree', *Journal of Applied Probability* 7, 79–88, nor the papers by A. J. Dobson, except Dobson (1969).

[73] The term 'glottochronology' is used here in this very wide sense.

[74] A percentage close to 80 has in fact been proposed. However, figures are cited here only by way of hypothetical example. On the notion of distance, see note 76.

[75] Sankoff (1973, 520, 523).

[76] Since a correlation is assumed for the sake of the argument, we use t both as a unit of time and as a unit of diversity ('distance'), however quantified, among languages. Incidentally, what represents time, graphically speaking, is not the length $\bar{z}$ of an edge as drawn in our rooted tree diagrams, but rather $\bar{z} \cdot \cos \alpha$, where α is the angle by which we let the edge deviate arbitrarily from the perpendicular time scale.

[77] In the special case of a no. 6 tree where $\bar{c} = \bar{a}$, the characteristics are, of course, $2\bar{a}$, $2\bar{a}$, $2\bar{a}$, as in Figure 84.

[78] This means that the distances and time depth for Y can be found.

[79] See Chapter II, Section 41.

[80] See Chapter II, Sections 4, 39.

[81] The matrices are taken from Hoenigswald (1966), where the manner in which the six trees can be generated out of IVa is set forth. IVa, with A, B, C, X, Y all kept separate, is the most general tree from the point of view of the comparative method.

INDEX OF TERMS AND SYMBOLS

FORMAL LINGUISTICS SERIES

Editor:

H. HIŻ, *University of Pennsylvania*

Consulting Editors:

ZELLIG S. HARRIS, *University of Pennsylvania*

HENRY M. HOENIGSWALD, *University of Pennsylvania*

Hum
P
25
F65
v.3

ANALYZED